US AIR FORCE
SPECIAL OPERATIONS
COMMAND

by Rick Llinares and Andy Evans

MDFX 1
US Air Force Special Operations Command
by Rick Llinares and Andy Evans

First produced in 2010 by SAM Limited, under licence from SAM Publications
Media House, 21 Kingsway, Bedford, MK42 9BJ, United Kingdom

ISBN 978-1-906959-21-0

Typeset by SAM Publications, Media House, 21 Kingsway, Bedford, MK42 9BJ, United Kingdom
Designed by Simon Sugarhood
Printed and bound in the United Kingdom by Buxton Press, United Kingdom

The MDF Series

- No.1 – De Havilland Mosquito *
- No.2 – Hawker Hurricane *
- No.3 – Supermarine Spitfire (Part 1: Merlin-Powered) *
- No.4 – Avro Lancaster (Inc Manchester & Lincoln)
- No.5 – Supermarine Spitfire (Part 2: Griffon-Powered)
- No.6 – Bristol Beaufighter *
- No.7 – English Electric Lightning
- No.8 – Gloster (& Armstrong-Whitworth) Meteor
- * Out of print

- No.9 – Messerschmitt Bf 109 (Part 1 Prototype to E Variants)
- No.10 – Messerschmitt Bf 109 (Part 2 F to K Variants)
- No.11 – British Aerospace Sea Harrier
- No.12 – The F-4 Phantom II (Part 1: USAF)
- No.13 – The F-4 Phantom II (Part 2: US Navy & Marine Corps)
- No.14 – The F-4 Phantom II (Part 3: Overseas Operators)
- No.15 – The Grumman F-14 Tomcat
- No.16 – The Hawker Hunter

Acknowledgments

Thanks are due to the following people for their help in the preparation of this title, and in no particular order, US Air Force Special Operations Command Public Affairs, US Air Forces Europe Public Affairs, RAF Mildenhall Public Affairs, Mark Smith, Michael Block and Steve Thompson.

The photographs that populate this work have been provided from the author's own collection and via various sources and third parties from around the world. Whilst every effort has been taken to ensure the correct permissions have been obtained to use these images, the publishers cannot accept responsibility for any ommissions beyond their control. Should any persons feel their copyright has been inadvertantly breached, this is wholly accidental, and they should contact the author via the publisher.

Andy Evans
June 2010

SAM PUBLICATIONS

Contents

The MH-53 'Pave Low'

The intimidating sight of an AC-130 Gunship

An atmospheric shot of the CV-22 *(© Rick Llinares)*

Introduction

The airmen and aircraft of the United States Air Force Special Operations Command are certainly amongst the elite of the aviation world. Flying some of the most unusual and powerful aircraft in the USAF inventory they provide a unique and hightly specialised service to the combat force.

the Air Force Special Operations Command (AFSOC) continues to provide an exceptional role within the service, and continues to fly some of the most distinctive aircraft in the world. Much has been written about the exploits of special operations aircraft in the Vietnam War, and also titles are available on individual aircraft types such as the AC-130, however this 'MDF Extra' brings together in one volume all of the special operations aircraft of today, either currently in service or recently retired, looking in detail at their operations, their variants and their combat roles. That is not to say that some small homage will not be paid to those aircraft types that have served with distinction in the past.

Rick Llinares Andy Evans
May 2010

A Combat Shadow flies into the sunset

MH-130 Combat Talon

Although the first use of 'Special Operations' came during World War II, it was possibly the Vietnam War which was the channel for the employment of clandestine aviation platforms, combined with the need to bring overwhelming surgical firepower to bear in a confined area, in bad weather, but more exactly under the cover of darkness. This led to the birth of the modern-day 'Gunship' in the shape of the elderly AC-47 'Spooky', followed by the AC-119 'Stinger' and the daddy of them all, the AC-130 Spectre. Allied to this came the MC-130 with its scissor nose, designed to pluck downed airmen from hostile territory, as well as the famous HH-3 'Jolly Green Giant' rescue helicopter and its 'Sandy' partner the A-1 Skyraider, that combined a powerful punch with a long loiter capability, and that made a formidable rescue team.

However it was the ill-fated 'Operation Eagle Claw' the attempt to recue American hostages fron the Embassy in Tehran that proved to be the catalyst that formed the dedicated Special Operations Command that exists today. Now in the 21st century

Special Operations, History and Overview

Chapter 1

A Fairchild AC-119 'Stinger' taxies out

AFSOC's mission is as 'America's specialised air power... a step ahead in a changing world, delivering special operations combat power anytime, anywhere'. The earliest Army Air Force Special Operations missions involved the 'Special Flight Section' of the 12th Air Force's 5th Bombardment Wing in North Africa, and their first combat mission was in October of 1943 in a modified B-17F. This small ad-hoc unit operated highly modified and mission unique B-17, B-24, and B-25 bombers from North Africa into France and other parts of occupied Europe and became known as the 885th Bombardment Squadron flying out of Brindisi, Italy. The largest Army Air Force effort in Europe was conducted by the 801st Bombardment Group nicknamed the 'Carpetbaggers', based in England and specialised in the delivery of supplies, agents, and leaflets behind enemy lines, using highly modified, unique, black painted B-24s.

Along with the conventional AAF troop carrier units, the special operations transports and bombers operating out of Brindisi, Italy, flew 3,769 successful sorties into the Balkans (79 percent to Yugoslavia). They dropped 7,149 tons of supplies to resistance groups while 989 C-47 landings behind enemy lines brought in another 1,972 tons. They also assisted in the evacuation of thousands of Allied airmen and wounded partisans during 1944-1945 and prior to, and during 'Operation Overlord', specially trained three-man Jedburgh teams were dropped behind enemy lines in France by Carpetbaggers and North African based units. Later, Carpetbaggers airlifted fuel to facilitate General Patton's armored drive out of France into

Germany. Another special operation, like the previous missions to Yugoslavia and under the code name 'Halyard Mission', extracted large groups of downed American airmen being protected by Yugoslav partisans. Between June and August 1944, OSS agents using Air Force C-47 transports landed behind enemy lines and recovered 432 Americans and eighty other Allied personnel.

In August 1943, General (Gen) Henry H. 'Hap' Arnold met with British Admiral Lord Louis Mountbatten to discuss plans for American air support of British commando expeditions in the China-Burma-India Theatre of Operations. General Arnold coined the term 'Air Commando' to honour Mountbatten who earlier commanded British commandos. By March 1944, the unit was designated the 1st Air Commando Group (1 ACG) and flew

The AC-47 saw combat use in Vietnam

The AC-47 colloquially known as 'Spooky'

over hazardous mountains and jungles to find and resupply the highly mobile British ground forces in hostile territory. It was from these missions that the 1 ACG earned its motto of 'Any Place, Any Time, Any Where', a variation of which is still used today. They used an array of aircraft including C-47 transports, P-51 and P-47 fighters, B-25 bombers, UC-64 utility aircraft, and a glider force of CG-4As and G-5s, augmented by R-4 helicopters. Special operations capabilities were mothballed in the demobilization after World War II. These capabilities were resurrected in the late 1940s as a means to help eliminate the Communist Huk insurgency in the Philippines.

The air power used to defeat the communist movement was organized along unconventional lines. Using United States (US) assistance under Lt Col Edward G. Lansdale, who in turn employed a Foreign Internal Defence (FID) mode of operation, the Philippine Air Force flew C-47s, P-51s, L-5s, AT-6 armed trainers, and a mixture of liaison aircraft against the Huks. Early in the Korean War, US Army intelligence and the fledgling Central Intelligence Agency (CIA), successor to the OSS, needed to deploy intelligence teams and supplies through short- and long-range low-level penetration into both North and South Korea. This involved the use of C-47 and C-119 transports, B-26 medium bombers, and Air Rescue Service crash boats. The Air Force then activated, equipped, and trained the 580th, 581st, and 582d Air Resupply and Communication Wings specifically for unconventional warfare and counterinsurgency operations.

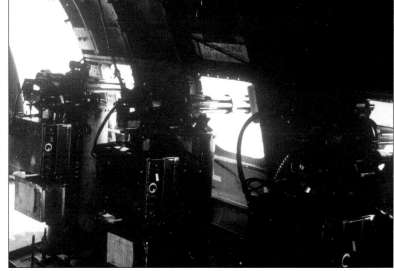

'Spooky' carried a mighty punch

These wings had tremendous capabilities using a variety of aircraft such as C-47, C-54, C-118, C-119 transports, B-29 bombers, SA-16 amphibians, and H-19 helicopters. General Curtis E. Le May, Air Force Chief of Staff, established the 4400th Combat Crew Training Squadron (CCTS) in April 1961.

Nicknamed 'Jungle Jim', the CCTS was based at Hurlburt Field, Florida, with a two-fold mission: counterinsurgency

Despite being a 'Dakota' the AC-47 provided a huge amount of firepower

The AC-47 paved the way for other such gunships

training and combat operations. Aircraft such as U-10s, C-46s, C-47s, B-26s, and AT-28s soon showed up on the Hurlburt flight line. In November 1961, the 4400 CCTS deployed a detachment to Bien Hoa, Republic of Vietnam, on 'Operation Farmgate' and thus, Air Force Special Operations Forces (SOF) flew some of the first US combat missions in Vietnam.

As the Vietnam War expanded, the Air Force increased its

An AC-119 in its Vietnam revetment

The 'sting' of the 'Stinger'

The HH-3 was one of the enduring sights of the Vietnam War

counterinsurgency capability. The 4400 CCTS became a group in March 1962, and the next month became part of the newly activated US Air Force Special Air Warfare Center (USAF SAWC) at Eglin Air Force Base (AFB), Florida. The Special Air Warfare Center obtained additional assets in the mid-1960s, to include O-1 and O-2 observation planes, A-26, A-37, and A-1 attack fighters, C-123, and later C-130 cargo aircraft, along with several types of helicopters. In addition to being outstanding short-field tactical transports, the C-123s were also modified as aerial sprayers for the 'Ranch Hand' defoliant missions in Vietnam. In 1964, air commandos deployed to Laos and Thailand on 'Operation Waterpump'. Also in late 1964, the first gunships were

introduced into combat with the deployment of AC-47 'Spooky' gunships to Vietnam.

The following year AC-119 'Stinger' and 'Shadow' gunships were introduced into combat, and by 1968 the first AC-130 'Spectre' gunships entered the Vietnam conflict. By the summer of 1968, the USAF SAWC was redesignated USAF Special Operations Force (USAFSOF) thus eliminating all reference to air commandos. At this time, the Vietnam War was at its peak and consumed virtually all of the Air Force's special operations efforts. One of the most notable missions supported by USAF special operations was the Son Tay prisoner of war (POW) camp raid in 1970, and the HH-3 'Jolly Green Giant' helicopter and the A-1 Skyraider were also making their mark as dedicated rescue and suppression platforms.

As the Vietnam War began winding down, SOF capability gradually declined as well. In June 1974, the USAFSOF was redesignated the 834th Tactical Composite Wing (TCW), effectively bringing to a close the most aggressive, far reaching

effort by the USAF to support unconventional warfare. In July 1975, the 834 TCW was renamed the 1st Special Operations Wing (1 SOW), and by 1979 it was the only SOF wing in the Air Force, comprising AC-130H 'Spectre' gunships, MC-130E 'Combat Talons', and CH-3E 'Jolly Greens' and UH-1N Huey helicopters. Two MC-130 'Combat Talon' squadrons remained overseas and the Air Force Reserve (AFRES) maintained the AC-130A gunship group and one HH-3E Jolly Green squadron.

When Operation 'Eagle Claw', the ill-fated attempt to rescue American hostages from the United States embassy in Iran ended in disaster at the Desert One refuelling site in April 1980, this proved a watershed for special operations forces. As a result, the Holloway Commission was convened and tasked to analyse why the mission failed and to recommend corrective actions, and thus began the gradual reorganisation and rebirth of United States Special Operations Forces. In October 1983,

Special Operations aircraft took part in the successful rescue of Americans from the island nation of Grenada. During the seven-day operation, MC-130s, AC-130s, and an EC-130 from the 193d Special Operations Group played significant roles. From late December 1989 to early January 1990, they took part in Operation Just Cause in Panama, and aircraft included AC-130 Spectre gunships, EC-130 Volant Solo psychological operations aircraft, HC-130P/N Combat Shadow tankers, MC-130E Combat Talons, and MH-53J Pave Low and MH-60G Pave Hawk helicopters.

On May 22, 1990, Gen Larry D. Welch, Air Force Chief of Staff, redesignated the unit as the Air Force Special Operations Command (AFSOC) which would now consist of three wings, the 1st, 39th and 353d Special Operations Wings, as well as the 1720th Special Tactics Group (STG), the US Air Force Special Operations School, and the Special Missions Operational Test and Evaluation Center and the AFRES components included the 919 SOG at Duke Field, Florida, and the 193 SOG of the ANG, located at the Harrisburg International Airport, Pennsylvania. From early August 1990 to late February 1991, AFSOC participated in Operations 'Desert Shield' and 'Desert Storm' employing AC-130s, HC-130s, MC-130s, MH-53s and MH-60s; the 193 SOG with its EC-130s; and the 919 SOG with its AC-130s and HH-3s, all deployed south of Kuwait. The 39 SOW deployed north of Iraq with its HC-130s, MC-130s, and MH-53s. Special tactics personnel operated throughout the theatre on multiple combat-control and combat-rescue missions.

AFSOC was heavily involved in the 1991 Gulf War and paid a high price for its operational tenacity when on 31 January 1991 an AC-130H was lost in combat while supporting coalition forces engaged in ground combat during the battle of Khafji. Following the Gulf War, AFSOC aircraft stood alert for personnel recovery and various other missions in support of Operations 'Provide

The ubiquitous HH-3, a welcome sight to many a downed airman

Quite a group: Skyraiders, a HC-130 and a Jolly Green

An MH-130 Pave Talon I with its Fulton recovery nose

An early AC-130 gunship

An AC-130A 'Plain Jane' of the 17th SOS taken in 1968

Comfort' and 'Southern Watch' as well as 'Provide Promise' and 'Deny Flight' the humanitarian relief effort and no-fly zone security in the Balkans. In January 1992, the 39 SOW relocated from Rhein-Main AB, Germany, to RAF Alconbury, and later that year was inactivated, and its personnel and equipment were reconstituted as the 352 SOW. In March 1994, the price of freedom and the high operations tempo was paid by a 16th Special Operations Squadron AC-130H gunship, call sign 'Jockey 14'. The aircraft was lost due to an in-flight explosion and ditching off the coast of Kenya while supporting Operation 'Continue Hope II' in Somalia. Eight crewmembers were killed,

six survived.

In early 1995, the 352 SOG relocated from RAF Alconbury to RAF Mildenhall, along with its supporting squadrons. Also during 1995, AFSOC was called on to support a number of peace keeping and humanitarian missions over Kosovo and in Somalia. AFSOC then began changing its readiness posture from one geared to countering the Soviet Union threat to one of co-operative engagements and peace enforcement activities, for which AFSOC forces' capabilities remained in constant demand. As part of Commando Vision, which started in 1994, the 919 SOW would not receive the AC-130Hs from the 16 SOW as had

A trio of MC-130s

An AC-130U fires a volley of flares

Replacing the MH-53 Pave Low is the CV-22 Osprey

An MC-130P fuels up a thirsty CV-22

The long arm of an MH-53 Pave Low

Operating Units

1st Special Operations Wing

The 1st SOW includes the 6th Special Operations Squadron (SOS), the 4th SOS, the 8th SOS, the 9th SOS, the 15th SOS and the 319th SOS. The 6th Special Operations Squadron is the wing's aviation foreign internal defence (FID) unit operating the UH-1N, Mi-8, C-130E, An-26 and C-47T; the 8th SOS now uses the CV-22 Osprey in place of its Pave Low's and 15th SOS employs the MC-130H Combat Talon, supporting unconventional warfare missions and special operations forces. The 9th SOS, at nearby Eglin AFB, flies the MC-130P Combat Shadow tanker for worldwide clandestine aerial refuelling of special operations helicopters, and the 4th SOS flies the AC-130U Spectre gunship. The 55th SOS was based at Hurlburt Field but with the arrival of the Osprey its MH-60G Pave Hawks were transferred to Air Combat Command. The recently formed 319th SOS flies the U-28A variant of the Pilatus PC-12 for intra-theatre support.

352nd Special Operations Group

The 352nd SOG at RAF Mildenhall, United Kingdom, is the designated Air Force component for Special Operations Command Europe. Its squadrons are the 7th SOS, which flies the MC-130H Combat Talon II and the 67th SOS, with the MC-130P Combat Shadow, and the 321st Special Tactics Squadron.

353rd Special Operations Group

The 353rd SOG, with headquarters at Kadena Air Base, Japan, is the Air Force component for Special Operations Command Pacific. The 353rd SOG is composed of the 1st SOS, flying the MC-130H and the 17th SOS flying the MC-130N/P

720th Special Tactics Group

The 720th STG, with headquarters at Hurlburt Field, FL, has special operations combat controllers, para-rescuemen, and combat weathermen who work jointly in Special Tactics Teams (STT). There are six Special Tactics Squadrons (STS) and one Combat Weather Squadron. The 320th STS at Kadena AB, Japan and the 320th STS at RAF Mildenhall, England are assigned to

A 'Super Jolly' en-route to a rescue during the Vietnam War

been planned. Instead the 919 SOW at Duke Field, Florida, retired its AC-130A gunships and gained MC-130P Combat Shadows, flown by the newly stood-up 5th SOS, and MC-130E Combat Talons, flown by the 711 SOS. During 2003 AFSOC was again heavily involved in Operation Iraqi Freedom and latterly in operations over Afghanistan.

and under the operational control of the 353rd and the 352nd Special Operations Groups respectively. The 720th also includes the 10th Combat Weather Squadron with headquarters at Hurlburt Field, FL, and detachments co-located with US Army Special Operations Command units.

27th Special Operations Wing

The 27th Special Operations Wing (27 SOW) is a wing of the United States Air Force stationed at Cannon Air Force Base, New Mexico. It is assigned to the Air Force Special Operations Command (AFSOC). The 27 SOW is the newest active-duty wing of AFSOC. The 27th SOW will take on strength the AC-130s from the 16th SOS from June 2010 and the CV-22 Ospreys from the 8th SOS. Also in-situ is the 73rd Special Operations Squadron which operates the latest in a long line of Hercules variants, the MC-130W 'Combat Spear', and is tasked with clandestine or low-visibility missions into denied areas to provide aerial refuelling to SOF helicopters or to air drop small SOF teams and supply bundles

58th Special Operations Wing

The 58th Special Operations Wing (58 SOW) is a combat unit stationed at Kirtland AFB in New Mexico. The 58 SOW serves as the premier training site for Air Force special operations and combat search and rescue aircrews. The wing operates eight different aircraft, these being the UH-1H, UH-1N, HH-60G, MH-53J, HC-130P/N, MC-130P, MC-130H, and CV-22 totalling more than sixty assigned aircraft. The wing teaches more than 100 courses in eighteen different crew positions including pilot, navigator, electronics warfare officer, flight engineer, communications system operator, loadmaster and aerial gunner.

Air Force Reserve and Air National Guard

During the special operations reorganisation AFSOC gained three Air Reserve Component units when mobilised. One is the

919th Special Operations Wing (AFRES) at Duke Field, FL that comprises the 711th SOS which flies the MC-130E Combat Talon I, while the 5th SOS flies the MC-130P Combat Shadow. The second unit is the 193rd Special Operations Group (ANG) at Harrisburg International Airport, which flies the EC-130E/J Commando Solo. The 919th SOW at Duke Field is the only Air Force Reserve special operations wing. When mobilised, it

reports to Air Force Special Operations Command. The 919th SOW trains Air Force reservists in MC-130E Combat Talon I and MC-130P Combat Shadow aircraft operations. Subordinate units of the 919th are the 711th SOS transitioned from the AC-130A Spectre gunship to the MC-130E Combat Talon I beginning in September 1995, and the 5th SOS which, activated in December 1994, flies the MC-130P Combat Shadow tanker.

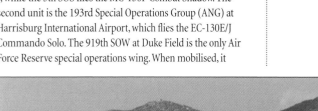
A UH-1 of the 6th SOS

A U-28A variant of the Pilatus PC-12

The Fairchild AC-119 was another success in the Vietnam War

The AC-130 Gunship 'Spooky and Spectre'

In 1967, JC-130A USAF 54-1626 was selected for conversion into the prototype AC-130A gunship

To quote an AC-130 pilot: "We destroy. No other words for it, our mission is to kill the enemy and destroy his equipment – and we are very good at it. We operate at night, when we are less vulnerable to optical sensors and carry a fair amount of self-defence kit, such as ECM and chaff and we pack a vicious punch! Based on the versatile Lockheed C-130 Hercules, the gunship version is a product of the Lockheed Aircraft Systems Company in Ontario, California. Built to meet an Air Force need during the Vietnam War, it was used extensively over the Ho Chi Minh Trail to find and destroy vehicles, and since its inception the 'Spectre' has matured into one of the most devastating and highly specialised aircraft on the USAF's inventory.

The AC-130A Gunship II superseded the AC-47 in the Vietnam War, and AFSOC currently uses both the AC-130H 'Spectre' and AC-130U 'Spooky' variants. Powered by four Rolls-Royce T56-A-15 turboprops the AC-130 has an armament ranging from 25mm Gatling cannons to an 105mm howitzer and carries a standard crew of twelve or thirteen airmen, including five officers (two pilots, a navigator, an electronic warfare officer and a fire control officer) and enlisted personnel (flight engineer, electronics operators, and aerial gunners). The US Air Force uses the AC-130 gunships for close air support, air interdiction, and force protection. Close air support roles include supporting ground troops, escorting convoys, and flying urban operations. Air interdiction missions are conducted against planned targets and targets of opportunity. Force protection missions include defending air bases and other facilities. Currently, AC-130U 'Spooky' model gunships are stationed at Hurlburt Field in Northwest Florida and the AC-130H 'Spectre' models are stationed at Cannon AFB, New Mexico.

In 1967, JC-130A USAF 54-1626 was selected for conversion into the prototype AC-130A gunship, and these

AC-130A of the 16th SOS at Ubon Air Force Base 1969

AC-130 Specifications

Engines	4 Allison turboprop engines T56-A-15
Dimensions	Length 29.8 m, Height 11.7 m, Wingspan 40.4 m
Max Takeoff Wt	69,750 kilograms
Range	1,300 nm (AC-130H) / 2,200 nm (AC-130U)
Ceiling	25,000 feet (AC-130H) / 30,000 feet (AC-130U)
Speed	300 mph (sea level)

CREW

AC-130H	AC-130U
14 crew consisting of:	13 crew consisting of:
• pilot	• pilot
• co-pilot	• co-pilot
• navigator	• navigator
• fire control officer.	• fire control officer.
• electronic warfare officer	• electronic warfare officer
• flight engineer	• flight engineer
• loadmaster	• loadmaster
• low-light TV operator	• all-light-level TV operator
• infrared detection set operator	• infrared detection set operator
• 5 aerial gunners	• 4 aerial gunners

COUNTERMEASURES

AC-130U:
- AN/AAQ-24 Directional infrared countermeasures (DIRCM)
- AN/AAR-44 Infrared warning receiver
- AN/AAR-47 Missile warning system
- AN/ALE-47 Flare and chaff dispensing system
- AN/ALQ-172 Electronic countermeasure system
- AN/ALQ-196 Jammer
- AN/ALR-69 Radar warning receiver
- AN/APR-46A Panoramic RF receiver
- QRC-84-02 Infrared countermeasures system

SENSORS

AC-130U:
- Multi-mode strike radar
- All-Light Level Television (ALLTV)
- Laser illuminator
- Laser designator
- Laser range finder

'Thor' showing its 'Black Crow' radome

modifications were done during that year at Wright-Patterson Air Force Base, by the Aeronautical Systems Division. A direct-view night-vision telescope was installed in the forward door, an early-style of forward looking infrared (FLIR) was fitted in the forward part of the left wheel well, and four Gatling guns fixed facing down and aft along the left side. The analog fire control computer prototype was handcrafted by RAF Wing Commander Tom Pinkerton at the USAF Avionics Laboratory. Flight testing of the prototype was subsequently performed primarily at Eglin Air Force Base, followed by further testing and modifications. By September 1967, the aircraft was certified ready for combat testing and was flown to Nha Trang Air Base, South Vietnam for a ninety-day test program.

Seven more AC-130 aircraft were converted to the 'Plain Jane' configuration like the AC-130 prototype in 1968, and one aircraft received the 'Surprise Package' equipment the next year. In 1970, an additional ten AC-130As were acquired under the 'Pave Pronto' project and conversion of C-130Es into AC-130Es for the 'Pave Spectre' project followed. 'Surprise Package' was equipped with the latest 20mm Gatling-style cannons and 40 mm Bofors cannon, but no

The AC-130 has been developed as a highly sophisticated side-firing weapons platform

A good plan view of the AC-130 is afforded here

7.62 mm close support armament, however this was retrofitted in the summer of 1970, and then the aircraft was redeployed to Ubon RTAFB. 'Surprise Package' served as a test bed for the avionic systems and armament for the AC-130E and in the summer of 1971 'Surprise Package' was converted to the 'Pave Pronto' configuration, and assumed its new nickname 'Thor'. In Vietnam, the gunships destroyed more than 10,000 trucks and participated in many crucial close air support missions. Various AC-130 versions following the Pave Pronto modifications were equipped with a magnetic anomaly detector (MAD) system called the Black Crow (AN/ASD-5), a highly sensitive passive device with a phased-array antenna located in the left-front nose radome that could pick up localized deviations in the Earth's magnetic field and was normally used to detect submerged submarines. The Black Crow system on the AC-130A/E/H could accurately detect the unshielded ignition coils of North Vietnamese

53-3129, affectionately dubbed 'The First Lady'

trucks that were hidden under the dense foliage of the jungle canopy along the Ho Chi Minh trail. It could also detect the signal from a hand-held transmitter that was used by air controllers on the ground to identify and locate specific target types. The system was slaved into the targeting computer. The PGM-38/U Enhanced 25 mm High Explosive Incendiary (HEI) round was created to expand the AC-130U gunship's mission in standoff range and survivability for its 25 mm GAU-12/U gun system. This round is a combination of the existing PGU-25 HEI and a M758 fuse designated as FMU-151/B to meet the MIL-STD-1316. The FMU-151 has an improved arming delay with multi-sensitive range.

The AC-130 Gunship first arrived in South Vietnam on 21 September 1967 under the Gunship II program, and began combat operations over Laos and South Vietnam that year. By 30 October 1968, enough AC-130 Gunship IIs arrived to form a squadron, the 16th Special Operations Squadron (SOS) of the 8th Tactical Fighter Wing (TFW), at Ubon Royal Thai Air Force Base, Thailand. By December 1968 most AC-130s were flown under F-4 Phantom II escort from the 479th Tactical Fighter Squadron, normally three Phantoms per Gunship. In late 1969, 'Surprise Package', 56-0490 arrived with solid state laser illuminated low light level TV with a companion YAG laser designator, an improved forward looking infrared (FLIR) sensor, video recording for TV and FLIR, an inertial navigation system, and a prototype digital fire control computer.

AC-130s also had a primary role during the invasion of Panama in 1989 for Operation Just Cause when they destroyed Panama Defence Force headquarters and numerous

command and control facilities. During the Gulf War of 1990-91 (Operations Desert Shield and Desert Storm), AC-130s provided close air support and force protection (air base defense) for ground forces, and battlefield interdiction. The primary interdiction targets were early warning/ground control intercept (EW/GCI) sites along the southern border of Iraq. The first gunship to enter the Battle of Khafji helped stop a southbound Iraqi armoured column on 29 January

1991. One day later, three more gunships provided further aid to Marines participating in the operation. The gunships also attacked Iraqi positions and columns moving south to reinforce their positions north of the city. Despite the threat of surface-to-air missiles and increasing visibility during the early morning hours of 31 January 1991, one AC-130H,

The more powerful AC-130U is equipped with the AN/APQ-180, synthetic aperture radar

AC-130A, 54-1630 'Azrael' now in the USAF Museum

A single 40mm Bofors gun is fitted, and is used against targets such as vehicles

The original rear guns on the AC-130A

Firing to 105mm Howitzer

An AC-130U fires off a volley of flares (© Rick Llinares)

target designator and rangefinder which gives deadly accuracy, and this is mounted on an AN/AJQ-24 stabilised tracking set. Also carried is an AN/APQ-150 Beacon Tracking radar and the powerful AN/AVQ-17 searchlight. Firepower comes from twin 20mm Gatling guns, a single 40mm gun and a huge 105mm Howitzer.

AC-130U 'The U-Boat'

The more powerful AC-130U is equipped with the AN/APQ-180, synthetic aperture radar for long-range target detection and identification. The gunship's navigational devices include INS systems and a Global Positioning System and it carries an integrated armour protection system (APS), high resolution sensors including an All Light Level Television (ALLTV), infrared detection set (IDS), upgraded avionics and EW systems, a sophisticated software-controlled fire control system, and an armament suite consisting of side-firing, trainable 25mm, 40mm, and 105mm guns. The

AF Serial No. 69-6567, call sign 'Spirit 03', opted to stay to continue to protect the Marines. A SAM subsequently shot down 'Spirit 03', and all fourteen crew members perished.

AC-130 were also used during the humanitarian operations in Somalia (Operation Restore Hope) and (operation United Shield) in 1992/1993, in the NATO mission in Bosnia-Herzegovina, and in 'Operation Silver Wake' in 1997, the evacuation of American non-combatants in Albania. During Operation 'Urgent Fury' (Invasion of Grenada) in 1983, AC-130s suppressed enemy air defence systems and attacked ground forces enabling the successful assault of the Point Salines Airfield. AC-130s have also played major roles in operation Iraqi Freedom and current operations over Afghanistan, where they continue to provide their own brand of air support.

AC-130H

The AC-130H is equipped with the Black Crow (AN/ASD-5), an AN/ASQ-145V low-light level television set (LLLTV) which allows nocturnal target acquisition, AN/AVQ-19 laser

APQ-180 strike radar provides the first gunship with the capability for all weather/night target acquisition and strike, and also provides extreme long-range target detection and identification and is able to track the 40mm and 105mm projectiles and return pinpoint impact locations to the crew for subsequent adjustment to the target. The fire control system offers a Dual Target Attack (DTA) capability, whereby two targets up to one kilometre apart can be simultaneously

An AC-130 showing the cheek fairings of the DIRCM system

When the 105 goes off it gives a pretty good jolt to the ship

Visible under the wheel sponson is the AC-130U's All Light Level TV (ALLTV) sensor

The AC-130U's fire control system offers a Dual Target Attack (DTA) capability *(© Rick Llinares)*

A superb underfuselage view of the AC-130U showing all the various sensors

The optics on the AN/AAQ-17 Infrared Detection Set (IDS) currently installed on the AC-130U, and the AC-130H will be brought up to the AN/AAQ-26 configuration

An AC-130U – 'U-Boat' taxies out (© Rick Llinares)

The AC-130U in flight

'Spooky'

engaged by two different sensors, using two different guns. The aircraft is also now pressurized, enabling it to fly at higher altitudes, saving fuel and time, and allowing for greater range than the AC-130H. Defensive systems include a countermeasures dispensing system that releases chaff and flares, and infra-red heat shields mounted underneath the engines disperse and hide engine heat sources from infra-red-guided anti-aircraft missiles. The optics on the AN/AAQ-17 Infrared Detection Set (IDS) currently installed on the AC-130U and AC-130H will be brought up to the AN/AAQ-26 configuration. The AC-130U has twice the munitions capacity of the AC-130H and can conduct some operations in daylight; however the majority of its combat missions are still conducted at night

In 2007, AFSOC initiated a program to upgrade the armament of existing AC-130s still in service, and this program called for the 25mm GAU-12/U and 40mm Bofors cannon on the AC-130U gunships to be replaced with two

30mm Mk.44 Bushmaster II cannons. The Air Force then modified four of their AC-130U gunships as test platforms for the Bushmasters. However, AFSOC cancelled its plans to install the new cannons on its fleet of AC-130Us and has since removed the guns and reinstalled the original 40mm cannons and returned the aircraft to combat duties. There are also plans to possibly replace the M102 howitzer with a breech-loading 120mm mortar, and to give the AC-130 a stand-off capability using either the AGM-114 Hellfire missile, the Advanced Precision Kill Weapon System (based on the Hydra 70 rocket), or the Viper Strike glide bomb. The Air Force also plans acquire sixteen new gunships based on modified, new-

build MC-130J special operations tankers that are outfitted with a 'precision strike package'. Some AC-130s are also now outfitted with the Directional Infrared Countermeasures (DIRCM) countermeasures system

Flying the 'Spectre'
A pilot's perspective of the AC-130H

"The AC-130 has been developed as a highly sophisticated side-firing weapons platform, designed to orbit a target, firing downward on to it, the idea being that the ordnance hits the centre of the circle, the target, and to complete its tasks the AC-130H is fitted with an impressive array of weaponry and sensors. These include two 20mm rotary `Gatling' guns, each capable of delivering 2,500 rounds per minute (which can be geared down to 2,000 rounds per minute) and primarily used for `soft' targets. A single 40mm Bofors gun is also fitted, firing 100 rounds per minute, and is used against targets such as vehicles. The most potent weapon on board is a single

An AC-130 dispatches its 40mm rounds

Darkness is the AC-130's friend!

105mm Army howitzer capable of dispatching between six and nine rounds per minute, and this is used to strike 'hard' targets such as buildings. These guns are all fitted on trainable hydraulic mounts and 'tied in' to the ship's sensors."

"This 'trainable mode' allows us to attack targets in close proximity, without the pilot having to adjust the aircraft's position, but we are also able to operate them in a 'fixed mode', which allows the pilot to acquire the target visually in an F-16 style HUD which is fitted to the left-hand window of his cockpit. The gun crews strive for a particular proficiency with their hand-loaded 105mms: they aim to have a shell in the breech, one on the way down and one hitting the target at any given time – 'driving nails', in gunship parlance. Because the howitzer points downward, the shell cases have to be specially crimped to stop them sliding down the barrel. Like the 105mm, which uses single rounds, the 40mm is also hand-loaded using four-round clips, and such is the appetite of the 20mm guns that one of the most important pieces of equipment aboard the Spectre is a 'snow shovel' to keep the spent cases from jamming up the breeches!"

"The 'brains' of the Spectre is the fire control system. It has two INS's, two fire control computers and a GPS, and these are tied into the Total Sensor Suite. This allows us to accurately navigate into an area and deliver our firepower (FCO, pronounced 'Foco'). Two gunners normally man the 20mms in the back, and a third serves as a 'right scanner' sitting just forward of 'the booth', which is gunship slang for the sensor suite compartment. Inside 'the booth' is the infra-red operator, a dedicated electronic warfare officer (EWO) and the LLLTV operator. In the aft cargo compartment are two more gunners who man the 40 and 105mm 'big guns', and finally, with his 'bubble' at the rear, is the loadmaster, whose duties in a combat situation include looking outside and below the aircraft for any threats."

"Before any combat mission there is an intensive briefing, where we look in as much detail as we can at our intended target or area of operations. The EWO is the recognised expert on all of the types of threat we could expect, and he will, together with the navigator, plot our best route. We take an Intel update and during our tasking evaluation we try to get a tight set of co-ordinates for our target so that we can be on station in the minimum time possible. We are performance-limited because we carry a lot of high-drag devices, either sticking out or hung under the wings, all of which make it heavier and more difficult to fly than a 'slick' C-130. Also we must be the only attack aircraft in the world that goes into combat without ejector seats! However, we do have on board our own parachutes, and we all wear a parachute harness, lifejacket, survival vest and flying helmets, with NVG attachments. The gunners wear Kevlar helmets that offer greater protection against blast problems."

"Once airborne, we need to do a sensor alignment, so we orbit the field at a nominal altitude, say 6,000 feet, picking a single point on the ground and tracking it with the visual sensors. We carry two basic types of sensor, 'visual' and 'electronic'. On the 'visual' side is the AN/AAD-7 FLIR, which is housed in a ball turret beneath the undercarriage bay. This gives a 360-degree view and is primarily used to locate targets en route, and we are able to slave it to the INS to get a really tight position. Once we have found the target and established our orbit, we switch to our other visual sensor, the AN/ASQ-145V low light level television (LLLTV), which is mounted on an AN/AJQ-24 stabilized tracking set and fitted with an AN/AVQ-19 laser target designator and rangefinder. This equipment is located in the crew entrance door. `The 'electronic' sensors comprise an AN/APQ150 beacon tracking

'Spectre'

Mission symbols from an AC-130 involved in Operation 'Iraqi Freedom'

The AC-130U has copious defensive aids including a countermeasures dispensing system that releases chaff and flares

A fully-laden AC-130U is a sobering sight!

Home at the end of another sortie

sensor, which is essentially a SLAB (sideways-looking airborne radar) that searches for and acquires radar beacons from friendly forces. Once located, the signal from the beacon allows us to accurately fly to its location. It is also able to transmit data to us, updating our target information. Second is the AN/ASD-5 'Black Crow' sensor, which can be tuned to frequencies such as those transmitted by truck ignition systems. Also fitted is an AN/APN-59B search radar system (AGMTIP) in the nose, complete with moving target indicator (MTI), and external illumination is provided by a 2kW AN/AVQ-17 searchlight mounted in the aft cargo area, and this is capable of 'normal' or infra-red operation. For self-defence we carry AN/ALE-20 chaff and flare dispensers fitted to the aft sections of the wheel bays, and wing-mounted SUU/42A pods which can each fire chaff and flares. Additionally we can carry externally hung AN/ALQ-87 ECM pods if necessary."

Looking directly underneath the AC-130U, and note the DIRCM sensors protruding from the front and rear fuselage

"The 'Foco' then aligns all of the ship's sensors to that point. He also checks that the pilot's HUD is correct for AGL, airspeed, and bank angle. Our next move is to 'tweak' the guns, which is a check to ensure the round will impact where the sensors are looking. What we do is find a remote place and then fire off a flare, to give us a fixed position to work with. A 'tweak' is one burst from each gun at 120-degree intervals, shooting three bursts from each gun in one orbit. On approach to the target area, we go to NVGs as the FLIR operator keeps a firm look-out to try and get an early target ID. Crew co-operation is a big part of Spectre operations, and primary conversations are on two separate networks, plus the main interphone to which everyone has access."

"About eight miles from the target we switch from 'En-Route Guidance' to 'Orbit Guidance', which will give us a tangent to the target as we roll in for our left-handed orbit around the area, using the attack mode segment of our orbit guidance system: this gives us a 'circle' of flight and shows us left or right, fore or aft of the target. Once those are centred up and we are close to the nominal bank angle for the orbit, I look through the HUD and get a 'diamond' superimposed over the target, which has now been acquired by the LLLTV operator, slewing his sensor around by using a 'thumbwheel' on his control panel. He 'sparkles' the target with laser energy, allowing us to get an accurate track, and that allows the fire control computer to calculate the exact range. With all of the sensors now looking at the same point on the ground, the guns are set to 'trainable mode', and these come up on their hydraulic mounts. The sensor operator then keeps the target firmly fixed in the cross-hairs on his TV screen."

"The Foco now works in concert with the two sensor operators, known simply as 'IR' or 'TV'; and he will have predetermined with them what he wants them to look for. The Foco then 'calls' the target once he is sure and has already planned to use our No 6 gun (the 105mm). I call 'Pilot in the

An AC-130U waits its turn to taxi in

The 'Big Stick', the 105mm Howitzer

'Loading the Brass'!

Feeding the 105mm howitzer

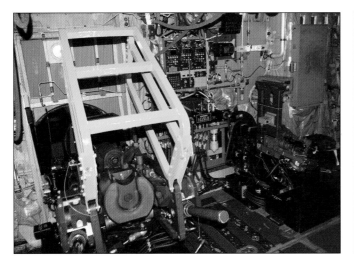

Down the breech of the 105! *(© Rick Llinares)*

Shell feed tubes to the voracious 25mm GAU-12/U *(© Rick Llinares)*

Looking pretty peaceful on the ground the AC-130 is devastating in the air!
(© Rick Llinares)

HUD, arm the gun!' The Foco will have the No.6 gun selected on his panel, so he flips all his switches and sets the correct ballistics into the computer. In conjunction with the navigator he again confirms the target and the flight engineer sets the master arm to 'Live'. In my HUD I get a CCIP (Constantly Computed Impact Point), and I have to keep that CCIP in the trainable box, which ensures that the target remains in the gun's correctable parameters, so even in high winds I can still adjust the orbit to enable us to fire all the way."

"When ready to shoot, I squeeze the trigger, and in 'trainable mode' this is the last electronic link to the sensor operator. When I have my finger on the trigger and all the constraints are met, he gets a 'Ready to fire' light on his panel. He pushes a button, which is a momentary consent switch, and this passes the firing pulse to the guns, with the computer constantly checking the rate and coincidence. As soon as the round is out, I come off the trigger and the gunners 'sling out the brass' and reload. They close the breech and call 'Gun ready'. I squeeze the trigger again. Meanwhile the sensor operators are looking at where the first round hits and making any adjustments for the next shell. When the 105 goes off it gives a pretty good jolt to the ship, but probably worse is a continuous burst from the 20mils. This leaves a lot of smoke floating around, even in the cockpit, but as we have so many open spaces on board it soon dissipates!"

An AC-130 comes in to land

An AC-130H in typical camouflage awaits its crew

Ground crews prepare to load supplies for a long flight! *(© Rick Llinares)*

The 'Phantom of the Ops! *(© Rick Llinares)*

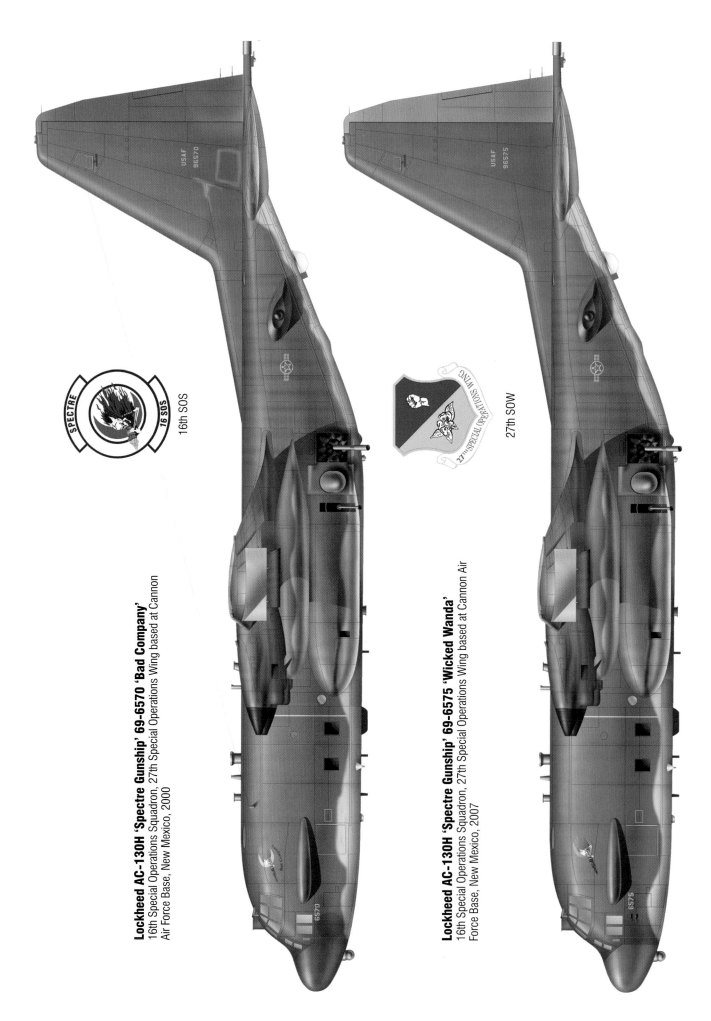

Lockheed AC-130H 'Spectre Gunship' 69-6570 'Bad Company'
16th Special Operations Squadron, 27th Special Operations Wing based at Cannon Air Force Base, New Mexico, 2000

16th SOS

Lockheed AC-130H 'Spectre Gunship' 69-6575 'Wicked Wanda'
16th Special Operations Squadron, 27th Special Operations Wing based at Cannon Air Force Base, New Mexico, 2007

27th SOW

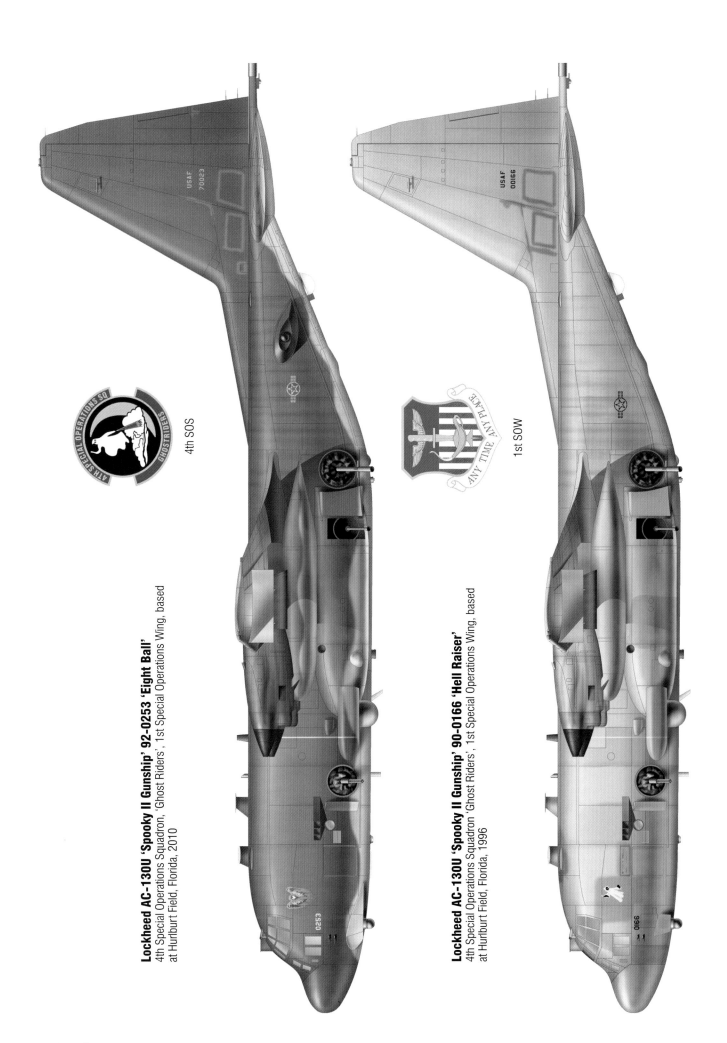

Lockheed AC-130U 'Spooky II Gunship' 92-0253 'Eight Ball'
4th Special Operations Squadron, 'Ghost Riders', 1st Special Operations Wing, based at Hurlburt Field, Florida, 2010

4th SOS

Lockheed AC-130U 'Spooky II Gunship' 90-0166 'Hell Raiser'
4th Special Operations Squadron 'Ghost Riders', 1st Special Operations Wing, based at Hurlburt Field, Florida, 1996

1st SOW

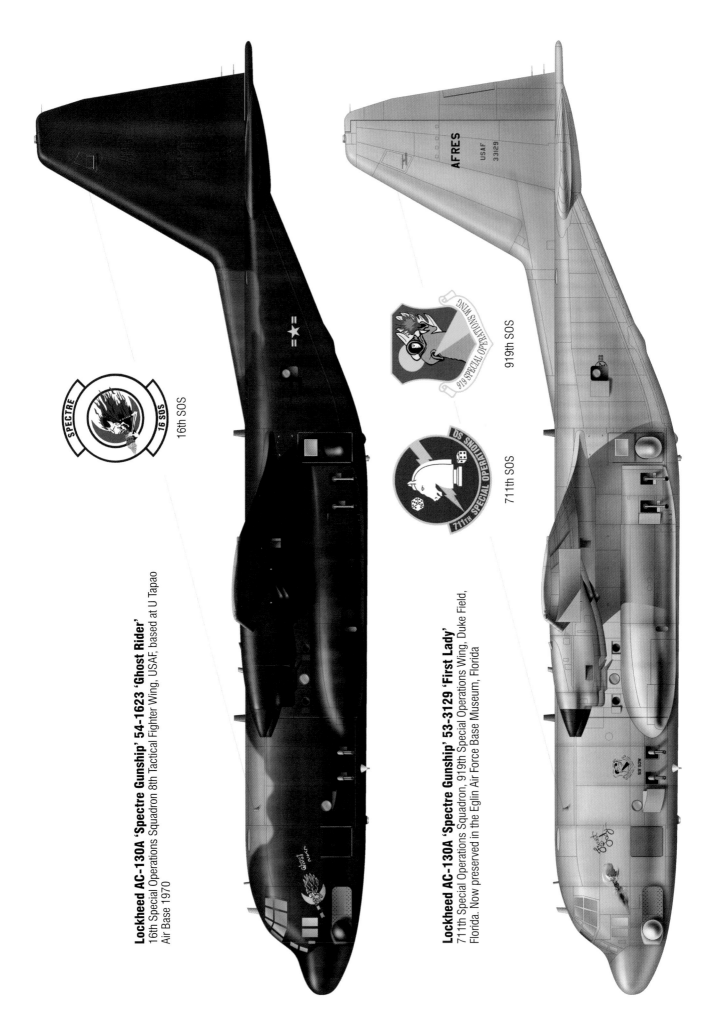

Lockheed AC-130A 'Spectre Gunship' 54-1623 'Ghost Rider'
16th Special Operations Squadron 8th Tactical Fighter Wing, USAF, based at U Tapao Air Base 1970

16th SOS

Lockheed AC-130A 'Spectre Gunship' 53-3129 'First Lady'
711th Special Operations Squadron, 919th Special Operations Wing, Duke Field, Florida. Now preserved in the Eglin Air Force Base Museum, Florida

919th SOS

711th SOS

The AC-130 Gunship
Walkaround

Super artwork! (© Rick Llinares)

The AC-13H's LLITV system (© Rick Llinares)

LLITV system in context with the aperture and DIRCM fairing (© Rick Llinares)

Starboard nose, note the box fairing for the FLIR (© Rick Llinares)

Looking upward at the cockpit and nose section (© Rick Llinares)

Note here the blast deflector above the hatchway (© Rick Llinares)

The FLIR of the AC-130H located under the wheel sponson

The business end of a 20mm on the AC-130H

The AN/AVQ-17 searchlight

AC-130 starboard side, seen during maintenance

Note the flexible aperture covering for the 25mm

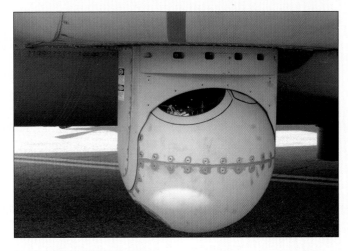

Close-in on the AC-130H FLIR ball

The fearsome 25mm Gatling gun (© Rick Llinares)

Upper fuselage appendages

Underfuselage vents

The 'big stick'! (© Rick Llinares)

The covering on the 105mm Howitzer (© Rick Llinares)

The AN/APQ-150 Beacon Tracking radar radome (© Rick Llinares)

40mm Bofors gun

AC-21A Note here the lack of AN/APQ-150 on the AC-130U (© Rick Llinares)

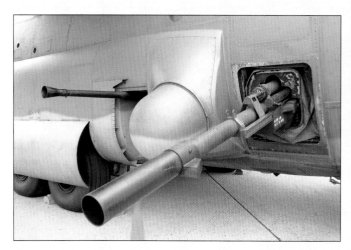

A 105mm fitted to the AC-130H

Looking at the frontal section of the exhaust IR heat-shielding

AC-21B Note the loaded chaff and flare dispensers here *(© Rick Llinares)*

Underfuselage antennae

Fin tip of an AC-130H

ECM fairing on the tail of an AC-130U

Tail ECM on the AC-130H

Engine IR heat-shield

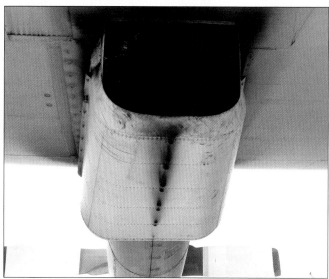

Looking directly up at the engine exhaust heat shielding

Wing antennae

The location of the 40mm and AN/APQ-150

'Spectre' *(© Rick Llinares)*

AC-130 – 'Hell's Shells!' *(© Rick Llinares)*

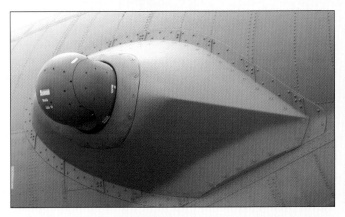

One of the rear fuselage-mounted DIRCM sensors

Looking at the frontal aspect of the rear fuselage DIRCM

An AC-130H carrying additional ECM and infra-red defeating pods

Inside the 'heart of the AC-130 (© Rick Llinares)

"The 'brains' of the Spectre is the fire control system. It has two INS's, two fire control computers and a GPS, and these are tied into the Total Sensor Suite *(© Rick Llinares)*

The 'office' *(© Rick Llinares)*

The MH-53 Pave Low

Chapter 3

During Operation 'Iraqi Freedom' the Pave Low played a vital role

MH-53 Pave Low was a modified version of the famous HH-53 'Super Jolly Green Giant', a heavy-lift helicopter which was used extensively during the Vietnam War. The MH-53's mission was to perform low-level, long-range, undetected penetration into denied areas, by day or night, and in adverse weather, for infiltration, exfiltration and resupply of special operations forces and rescue missions. The USAF's 'Super Jollies' were useful helicopters, but they were essentially daylight/fair weather machines, and downed aircrew were often in trouble at night or in bad weather. A limited night/foul weather sensor system designated 'Pave Low I' based on a low-light-level TV (LLLTV) imager was deployed to Southeast Asia in 1969 and combat-evaluated on a 'Super Jolly', but reliability was not adequate. In 1975, an HH-53B was fitted with the much improved 'Pave Low II' system and redesignated YHH-53H. This exercise proved much more acceptable, and so eight HH-53Cs were given a further improved systems fit and redesignated HH-53H 'Pave Low III', with the YHH-53H also being upgraded to this specification, and all were delivered during 1979 and 1980. The first nine Pave Lows became operational July 1, 1980, however they were transferred from the Military Airlift Command, where they were to have been CSAR assets, and assigned to the 1st Special Operations Wing in the aftermath of the Operation 'Eagle Claw' disaster. Two of their number were lost in training accidents in 1984, and thus a pair of CH-53C 'Pave Knife' aircraft, which had already gained fame in a number of incidents including Operation 'Frequent Wind' were brought

The MH-53 is certainly an imposing sight

Seen here is its 1990's color scheme

Fast roping from a Pave Low

Firing a volley of flares

A pair of Pave Lows' kick up sand and debris during a beach-head sortie

A superb air-to-air shot of the now retired Pave Low
(© Rick Llinares)

Note the IFT probe
(© Rick Llinares)

The unmistakable frontage of the MH-53 Pave Low

up to Pave Low standard as replacements.

The HH-53H retained the in-flight refuelling probe, external fuel tanks, rescue hoist, and three-gun armament of the HH-53C; and armament was typically a mini-gun on each side of the fuselage and a Browning .50cal gun in the tail to provide more reach and a light anti-armour capability, however crews were at pains to point out that despite the firepower, they were not gunships!. Other improvements included a Texas Instruments AN/AAQ-10 forward-looking infra-red (FLIR) imager, an AN/APQ-158 terrain-following radar (TFR), which was a digitised version of the radar used by the A-7 Corsair further modified to be able to give terrain avoidance and terrain following commands simultaneously, a Marconi Doppler-radar navigation system, Litton INS, a computerised moving-map display, a radar-warning receiver and AN/ALQ-157 IRCM pods strapped to the outer fuel tank sponsons, as well a copious chaff-

flare dispensers. The FLIR and TFR were mounted on a distinctive 'chin' fairing. "You have to learn to trust the TF/TR" explained a Pave Low pilot. "Watching the climb and dive commands takes a certain concentration, especially in the dark!" The Pave Low could also be fitted with twenty-seven seats for troops or fourteen litters. In 1986, the surviving HH-53Hs were given an upgrade under the 'Constant Green' program, featuring incremental improvements such as a cockpit with blue-green lighting compatible with NVG's, and they were also then reclassified as 'special operations' machines and accordingly given a new designation of MH-53H.

As the HH-53H proved itself, the Air Force decided to order more, coming up with an MH-53J 'Pave Low III Enhanced' configuration. This was similar to that of the HH-53J, the major change being fit of twin T64-GE-415 turbo-shaft engines as well as more armour, and there were some avionics upgrades as well, including a GPS satellite navigation receiver. A total of thirty-one HH-53Bs, HH-53Cs, and CH-53Cs were upgraded to the MH-53J configuration from 1986 through 1990, with all MH-53Hs upgraded as well, providing a total of forty-one MH-53Js. The MH-53M Pave Low IV was a further modified MH-53J with the Interactive Defensive Avionics System/Multi-Mission Advanced Tactical Terminal or IDAS/MATT which enhanced the existing

Coming in 'hot' *(© Rick Llinares)*

The FLIR and TFR mounted on a distinctive 'chin' fairing

A good rear underside view here

The MH-53J was powered by twin T64-GE-415 turbo-shaft engines

Note the lack of a nosewheel door

Maintenance work being undertaken on one of the MH-53 power plants

Fast roping at sea

MH-53 Pave Low was a modified version of the famous HH-53 'Super Jolly Green Giant'

The huge rotor blades stir up debris as the Pave Low comes to a hover

The Pave Low could also be fitted with twenty-seven seats for troops or fourteen litters *(© Rick Llinares)*

The MH-53, with its replacements – CV-22 Ospreys! *(© Rick Llinares)*

Hovering in the dark the Pave Low makes an impressive spectacle!

A night pairs take-off

defensive capabilities of the aircraft and provided instant access to the total battlefield situation, through near real-time Electronic Order of Battle updates. It also included a new level of detection avoidance with near real-time threat broadcasts over-the-horizon, so crews could avoid and defeat threats, and replan en-route if needed.

MH-53Js were used in a variety of missions during 'Desert

Flying low over the coast
(© Rick Llinares)

Storm' and Pave Lows were among the first aircraft into Iraq when they led Army AH-64 Apaches to destroy Iraqi early-warning radars and opened a hole in enemy air defences for the air armada to funnel through. In addition to infiltration, exfiltration and resupply of Special Forces teams throughout Iraq and Kuwait, Pave Lows provided search and rescue coverage for coalition air forces in Iraq, Saudi Arabia, Kuwait, Turkey and the Persian Gulf. An MH-53J made the first successful combat recovery of a downed pilot in Desert Storm, and following the war MH-53Js were deployed to Northern Iraq to support Operation 'Provide Comfort', assisting displaced Kurds. Pave Lows were also used extensively during Operation 'Just Cause' in Panama and were also instrumental in recovering USAF F-16 pilot Scott O'Grady during the Balkans/Kosovo campaign. The helicopters also played vital roles in Operation 'Iraqi Freedom'. The MH-53 'Pave Low's' last mission was on 27 September 2008, when the remaining six helicopters flew their last combat missions in support of special operations forces in south west Asia. These MH-53Ms were retired in September 2008 and replaced by the CV-22 Osprey, and dating back to their days as the HH-53 in the Vietnam War (a famous group of five such aircraft taking part in 'Operation Kingpin' – the rescue of American POWs from Son Tay prison near Hanoi), these aircraft have served with great distinction.

A total of thirty-one HH-53Bs, HH-53Cs, and CH-53Cs were upgraded to the MH-53J configuration *(© Rick Llinares)*

A Browning .50cal gun was fitted in the tail to provide more reach and a light anti-armour capability

The MH-53 'Pave Low's' last mission was on 27 September 2008 *(© Rick Llinares)*

The sheer size of the MH-53 would have been a welcome sight to any downed airman!

A superb high angle shot of a Pave Low (© Rick Llinares)

In the heat of the Iraqi desert a technician works on his Pave Low

Pave Lows provided search and rescue coverage for coalition air forces in Iraq (© Rick Llinares)

A Pave Low waits for its crew
(© Rick Llinares)

The MH-53 Pave Low during a low-level training exercise

MH-53J's were used in a variety of missions during 'Desert Storm' *(© Rick Llinares)*

The IFR, FLIR and radar *(© Rick Llinares)*

In its hangar for much needed maintenance *(© Rick Llinares)*

Coming in close! *(© Rick Llinares)*

The enormous power of the MH-53 is evident here, as the loadmaster hangs out of the cabin door providing a commentary to the pilot as he lowers the huge helicopter onto an aircraft carrier's rolling deck *(© Rick Llinares)*

A Pave Low plugs into the 'basket' of a Combat Shadow in order to extend its range on task *(© Rick Llinares)*

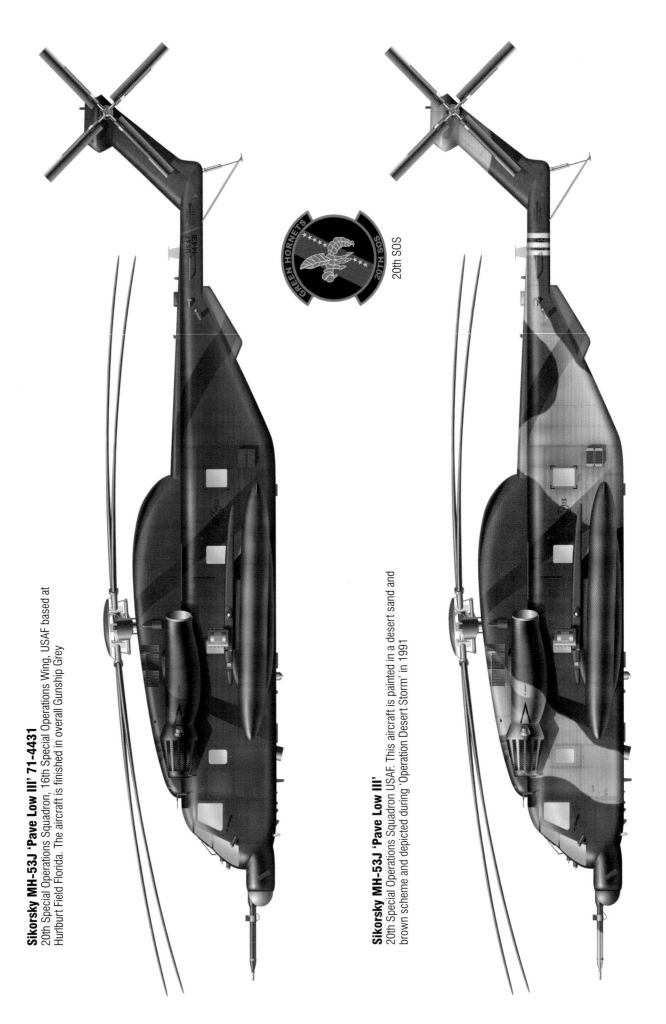

Sikorsky MH-53J 'Pave Low III' 71-4431
20th Special Operations Squadron, 16th Special Operations Wing, USAF based at Hurlburt Field Florida. The aircraft is finished in overall Gunship Grey

Sikorsky MH-53J 'Pave Low III'
20th Special Operations Squadron USAF. This aircraft is painted in a desert sand and brown scheme and depicted during 'Operation Desert Storm' in 1991

20th SOS

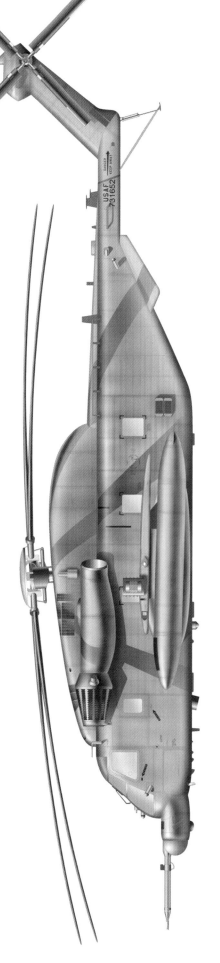

Sikorsky MH-53J 'Pave Low III' 68-8284
21st Special Operations Squadron, 352nd Special Operations Group USAFE based at RAF Alconbury, England 1992. The aircraft is painted in a three tone European scheme of dark grey, dark green and medium green

Sikorsky MH-53M 'Pave Low IV' 73-1652
20th Special Operations Squadron, 16th Special Operations Wing, USAF based at Hurlburt Field Florida, and depicted here during the final year of MH-53 operations, serving in Iraq. The aircraft is painted in an overall medium grey scheme

21st SOS

The MH-53 Pave Low
Walkaround

The frontal aspect of the MH-53J

AN/ALQ-157 mounting without pod

IFR Probe

Looking down inside the Pave Low cabin

The fairing for the AN/APQ-158 terrain-following radar

Note here the box-fairing added to accommodate the extra systems

Tail-boom-mounted SATCOM aerial

External fuel tank – front to rear

Side-mounted fuel tank on sponson – rear to front aspect

Forward fuselage showing cockpit glazing

Sponson-mounted AN/ALQ-157 IRCM pod

Rescue hoist and lighting

Engine intake cover and rescue hoist

Rotor hub

Rear ramp showing wind deflector and ECM bulges

Underfuselage chaff and flare dispenser

The AN/AAQ-10 forward-looking infra-red (FLIR) imager

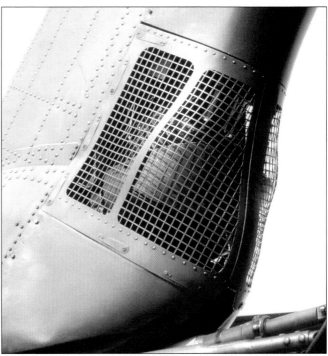

Tail boom grille

The pilots' 'office'

The MC-130 Combat Talon

Chapter 4

Close-in on the pivot point of the 'Fulton Nose'

Combat Talon I

The MC-130E Combat Talon I was originally developed to support clandestine special operations missions during the Vietnam War and eighteen such aircraft were created by modifying C-130Es, and although four were lost through attrition the remainder continued in service more than four decades after their initial modification. The updated Combat Talon II was developed in the 1980s and likewise four of the

In 1964 Lockheed had modified six C-123B Providers for unconventional warfare under Project 'Duck Hook' and then been tasked with adapting the C-130E, when the 'Duck Hook' aircraft proved inadequate. The modifications under 'Thin Slice' and its August 1966 successor 'Heavy Chain' were further code-named 'Rivet Yard', and the four C-130Es came to be known as 'Yards'.

An unusual sight – the 'duckbill' radome pulled forward to reveal the avionics inside

An early MC-130 with the 'Fulton Nose' and velvet black and green scheme which resulted in the aircraft being nicknamed 'Blackbirds'

original twenty-four aircraft have been lost in operations.

The Combat Talon was initially developed between December 1964 and January 1967 by Lockheed Air Services (LAS) at Ontario, California, as the result of a study by 'Big Safari', the USAF's office responsible for modification and sustainment of special mission aircraft. Two highly classified test bed aircraft, 64-0506 and 64-0507, were assigned to Project 'Thin Slice' to develop a low-level clandestine penetration aircraft suitable for Special Forces operations in Southeast Asia.

As the 'Thin Slice' aircraft were being developed, SOG requirements resulted in the procurement of fourteen similarly modified aircraft in 1965, and the first of these aircraft were diverted to Lockheed's facility in Marietta, Georgia, in December 1965 for installation of the Fulton STARS (then ARS) system, at the rate of three aircraft per month. While awaiting installation of the ARS equipment, other C-130s were ferried to Greenville, South Carolina, for painting by Ling-Temco-Vought Electrosystems with a low-radar-reflective paint that added 370 pounds to their weight. The velvet black and green scheme resulted in the aircraft being nicknamed 'Blackbirds'. As the installation was completed, the 'Blackbirds' were returned to Ontario for installation of the electronics package, code-named 'Rivet Clamp'. The aircraft collectively were then assigned the designation Combat Talon in 1967. The Fulton STARS

A 'Blackbird' MC-130 lumbers out

equipment was, however, removed from all Combat Talons during 1998. The 'Rivet Clamps', originally designated C-130E(I), were equipped with an electronic and infrared (IR) countermeasures suite and the AN/APQ-115 navigational radar adapted from the AN/APQ-89 radar used in the RF-4C Phantom and featured terrain-following/terrain-avoidance (TF/TA), Doppler, and mapping radar modes, and enabled it to operate at low altitudes, at night and in all-weather conditions, and avoid known enemy radar and anti-aircraft weapons concentrations.

Beginning in 1970, Texas Instruments and Lockheed Air Service worked to adapt the existing AN/APQ-122 Adverse Weather Aerial Delivery System (AWADS) with terrain-following/terrain-avoidance modes to replace the original APQ-115, and in 1970 they succeeded, and coupled the APQ-122 with the Litton LN-15J Inertial Navigation System (INS). Known as MOD-70, the modified radar was installed in all twelve operational Combat Talon and the four 'Heavy Chain' test beds between 1971-1973. The system proved so successful that it continued in service until the late 1980s. Following the completion of MOD-70, the Combat Talons were divided into three designations: C-130E(CT) for the 'Clamp' aircraft,

C-130E(Y) for the 'Yank' and C-130E(S) for the 'Swap'. The Combat Talon designations were consolidated in 1977 under the aegis of the 'MC-130' and have remained under that designation ever since. The Combat Talon became the 'Combat Talon I' in 1984 with the authorisation for the modification of twenty-four C-130Hs to Combat Talon II specifications. The 'Yank' Talons conducted top secret operations worldwide, under the project name 'Combat Sam', until late 1972 and two of the original 'Clamps' were lost in combat in Southeast Asia

An MC-130E in three-tone tactical camouflage

Great artwork on this MC-130

'Merlins Magic' with its
replacement radome featuring
a FLIR mounting

An MC-130E positions to take
on gas

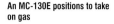

and were replaced by two C-130Es and these remained as
Combat Talons until 1972, when 'Heavy Chain' was gradually
discontinued and its four aircraft were integrated into the
Combat Talon force. The two original 'Thin Slice' aircraft were
given the serials of two destroyed C-130s, 62-1843 and 63-7785
respectively, to disguise their classified origins, and these
replacements had their modifications removed and were
returned to airlift duties, although known as 'Swaps' they

remained available for future Combat Talon use.

All fourteen 'Combat Talon Is' had upgraded navigational
radars, an enhanced electronic warfare suite and were provided
with new outer wings, and by 1995 were equipped with
helicopter-air-refuelling pods. The 'Combat Talon I' first saw
operational action in the Vietnam War, beginning September 1,
1966 under a deployment known as 'Combat Spear', which
preceded operational deployment of other Combat Talons to
Europe under 'Combat Arrow' and the US under 'Combat Knife'.
In 1974 the Combat Talon program was nearly dismantled as the
Air Force sought to reverse its Vietnam emphasis on special
operations and the 1st Special Operations Wing was redesignated
the 834th Tactical Composite Wing and its Combat Talons of the
8th SOS became a TAC asset. However the use of 1st SOS 'Yank'
Talons in a sea-surveillance role off North Korea in 1975 revived
interest in the Combat Talon, as did the Israeli hostage rescue at
Entebbe Airport. By November 1979, the Combat Talon force was
divided among three squadrons, the first two of which were
operationally deployed, and the third at Hurlburt essentially the
force training squadron.

Following the seizure of the US embassy in Tehran, Iran, in
November 1979, training operations for a rescue mission of the
fifty-three hostages was undertaken. Operation 'Eagle Claw'
was started and four Combat Talons (including a spare) of the
1st SOS staged to Masirah Island off the coast of Oman on April
19, 1980, to lead the 'Night One' infiltration phase, while the

three of the 8th SOS deployed to Wadi Qena, Egypt, on April 21 to lead the 'Night Two' exfiltration phase. Although the mission was an embarrassing failure costing eight lives, seven helicopters, and an EC-130E aircraft in a ground accident, the MC-130s performed nearly flawlessly. Planning initiatives for a second rescue attempt, under the project name 'Honey Badger', began two weeks after the failed raid and continued through November. Combat Talon participation in 'Honey Badger' amounted largely to tactics development, but ECM improvements included chaff and flare dispensers and new ALR-69 threat receivers that improved its defensive countermeasures capability well beyond that existing prior to 'Eagle Claw'.

Five Combat Talons of the 8th Special Operations Squadron participated in Operation 'Urgent Fury', the United States invasion of Grenada between October 25 and 31, 1983, with five Combat Talons, divided into three elements, with two of these leading formations of Special Operations Low Level-equipped (SOLL) C-130 transports. Combat Talons also supported Operation 'Just Cause', the invasion of Panama in December 1989 and January 1990 when three MC-130Es airlanded Rangers of the 2nd Battalion 75th Ranger Regiment into Rio Hato Military Airfield and the operation was conducted under total blackout conditions, using night-vision goggles. The 1991 invasion of Kuwait by Iraq resulted in the deployment of four Combat Talons and six crews of the 8th SOS in August 1990 to King Fahd International Airport in Saudi Arabia as a

component of Operation 'Desert Shield', and during Operation 'Desert Storm' in 1991, the Combat Talon performed one-third of all airdrops and participated in psychological operations, flying leaflet-drop missions before and throughout the war. Combat Talon crews also conducted five BLU-82B 'Daisy Cutter' missions during the two weeks preceding the onset of the ground campaign, dropping eleven bombs on Iraqi positions at night from altitude. Two 7th SOS Talons deployed to Incerlik Air Base, Turkey, as part of Operation 'Proven Force'

A great underside view showing all the ECM equipment associated with the DIRCM

Tanking from a KC-135, note the 'Fulton Nose'

Low over the sea, a Combat Talon I fires off a volley of flares

An MC-130H Combat Talon II from 'above' *(© Rick Llinares)*

where they supported the first Joint Search and Rescue mission over Iraq, attempting to recover the crew of 'Corvette 03', a downed F-15E Strike Eagle. On October 6, 1995, the Air Force began shifting the 'Combat Talon I' force to the Air Force Reserve Command's 711th Special Operations Squadron based at Duke Field, Florida, with the transfer of MC-130E 64-0571. Six went to the 711th SOS over the next year for crew training,

and the squadron became operational on March 1, 1997. On March 5, 1999, the 8th SOS became the first active force squadron to become an Associate Unit to an Air Reserve Component organisation, co-located with the 711th SOS, but without aircraft of its own, flying those of the reserve unit. A 'Combat Talon I' was the first aircraft to land at New Orleans International Airport after Hurricane Katrina in August 2005 and on July 14, 2006, the 8th SOS flew its last 'Combat Talon I' mission before converting to the CV-22 Osprey.

Combat Talon II

The first fully operational MC-130H 'Combat Talon II' -87-0024 was received by the 8th SOS on June 29, 1991, with three others delivered in the summer, and by December 1991 the 8th SOS was equipped with six aircraft. 'The Combat Talon II' featured a stronger airframe and modifications to the rear and aft cargo doors. The electronics suite had been upgraded, to include GPS navigation, special radars for navigating in adverse weather, and an NVG capability. These new technologies allowed the 'Combat Talon II' to fly as low as 250 feet above ground level

Five Combat Talons of the 8th Special Operations Squadron participated in Operation 'Urgent Fury'

Caught at the moment a flare is fired from one of the dispensers in front of the side access door

(AGL) in inclement weather, and make faster, more accurate airdrops. Increases in automation also reduced the aircrew by two. Initial Operational Capability was reached on June 30, 1993. Three MC-130H 'Combat Talon IIs' of the 7th SOS were deployed in December 1995 to deliver peacekeeping forces to Tuzla and Sarajevo, Bosnia and Herzegovina, as part of Operation 'Joint Endeavor', during which one Talon was hit by ground fire. The first combat deployment of a 'Combat Talon II' was on April 8, 1996, during Operation 'Assured Response' where special operations forces were deployed to Liberia to assist in the evacuation of 2000 civilians from the American embassy when the country broke down into civil war.

'Combat Talon II' deployments for joint exercises in 1997 included Australia, Guam, Indonesia, South Korea, and Thailand, and in July 1997 three 'Talon IIs' deployed to Thailand as part of Operation 'Bevel Edge', the proposed rescue of 1,000 American citizens trapped in Phnom Penh, Cambodia, but the crisis ended when the government allowed all non-citizens who wanted to, to leave by commercial aircraft. Full Operational Capability for the 'Combat Talon II' was reached in February 2000 and at that time twenty-four MC-130Hs were

deployed to four squadrons, these being with the 15th SOS at Hurlburt Field, the 1st SOS at Kadena, the 7th SOS at RAF Mildenhall and the 550th SOS at Kirtland AFB. On the night of October 19-20, 2001, four 'Combat Talon IIs' infiltrated a task force of 199 Rangers of the 3rd Battalion 75th Ranger Regiment and tactical PSYOP teams 658 miles inside Taliban-held Afghanistan where the force dropped onto 'Objective Rhino' an

The sheer brute power of the Herc is evident here

The Talon II carries a crew of seven, two fewer than the Talon I

Tucking its wheels up, an MC-130 Combat Talon II gets airborne

Note here the removed 'Fulton' gear from the nose of this 'Talon'

unused airfield in Kandahar Province 110 miles south-west of Kandahar, to secure a landing zone as a temporary operating base for Special Forces units conducting raids in the vicinity. A month later, two MC-130Hs, flying from Masirah Island, inserted US Navy SEAL Team Three and four HMMWV vehicles to within ten miles of the same airfield on the night of November 20-21. 'Combat Talon IIs' of the 7th SOS, augmented by crews from the 15th and 550th SOSs, flew 13-15-hour airdrop and airlanding night resupply missions from Incirlik

Air Base, Turkey, to Special Forces Operational Detachments-Alpha (ODAs) in Afghanistan during the opening phase of Operation 'Enduring Freedom' in December 2001. Operating in mountainous terrain, they produced an airdrop tactic by replicating maximum-effort landing techniques to rapidly descend from 10,000 ft (3,000 m) to 500 ft (150 m) AGL to ensure accurate gravity drops after clearing high ridgelines into deep valleys.

The 7th SOS conducted many sorties during Operation 'Iraqi

Freedom' in 2003. The 7th SOS was attached to the Joint Special Operations Task Force - North, known as 'Task Force Viking', whose objective was to hold thirteen Iraqi Army divisions along the 'Green Line' in north-eastern Iraq to prevent those divisions from reinforcing other Iraqi operations against US forces invading from Kuwait. On March 22, six 'Combat Talon IIs' completed a fifteen-hour mission, the longest in US Special Operations history, inserting troops into Iraq, a mission that consisted of a four and one-half hour low-level flight at night through western and northern Iraq to Bashur and Sulaymaniyah airfields, often taking heavy ground fire from the integrated air defences. The Talon IIs, at emergency gross weight limits, operated blacked-out, employed chaff and electronic countermeasures, flew as low as 100 ft, and carried their troops tethered to the floor of the cargo holds. Three of the Talons were battle-damaged, with one forced to land at Incirlik Air Base. The operation became known informally as 'Operation Ugly Baby'. After airlanding their troops, the Talon IIs then had to fly back through the alerted defences to recover to their launching point.

The 'Duckbill' radome of the Combat Talon II

Being marshalled in at Mactan Air Base

Undergoing maintenance

With its different nose this MC-130E gets airborne

Operating the Combat Talon II

"With due deference to the AC-130 attack and EC-130 electronic versions of the Hercules, the MC-130 flies the most demanding of mission profiles for such a large aircraft, moving in hostile environments and undertaking clandestine operations", explains an MC-130E Combat Talon II pilot. "Our role is global, by day, night or in adverse weather, and we have the ability to air-drop personnel and equipment, infiltrating or exfiltrating Special Forces and keeping them supplied in sensitive or politically denied areas. The MC-130 possesses some very high-tech equipment to fly these missions, and it is instantly distinguishable from other 'Hercs' by its unusual 'Duckbill' radome, which houses an AN/APQ-170 multi-mode radar, with ground mapping and terrain-avoidance/terrain-

following capabilities. This allows the Combat Talon to fly very low, 'picking holes through the terrain and threading through the weather.'"

"The MC-130 has a 'glass cockpit' and all the flight-deck work stations each have two video display terminals (VDT) together with data entry keyboards. Integral to each VDT are twenty-one variable-function, software-controlled switches positioned around the outsides. Key legends are shown on each VDT next to each switch, to indicate the current mode being displayed. The five switches along the top are for primary display modes, while the eight on either side provide the appropriate selection mode. In the cockpit both pilot and co-pilot have two VDTs as well as the more traditional 'needles and dials'. These VDTs can show primary flight instrumentation as

The MC-130 possesses some very high-tech equipment to fly its missions

With its DIRCM appendages on the rear fuselage in evidence this MC-130H holds for its turn on the runway

well as situational data. There are several varieties of vertical display formats for control of the aircraft, its guidance and flight information, with horizontal displays presenting tactical, radio and navigational data. These formats are available with symbology alone or can be overlaid with radar or FLIR information."

"The MC-130 is built by Lockheed as a basic shell, with IBM Federal Systems Division handling the systems integration and E-Systems installing all the specialised avionics. For the degree of accuracy called for by its mission, the MC-130 has a dual INS and GPS which will be updated by an AN/ARN-92 LORAN-C. For the resupply function it is fitted with a Low-Level Aerial Delivery and Container Release System, tied to a computer-controlled release point. Bad weather and night operations are further aided by the installation of a FLIR fitted in a ball turret beneath the radome and enabling the crew to see the world outside on their green screens. Self-protection is enhanced by a large number of AN/ALE-40 chaff and flare launchers mounted on the wing pylons, fuselage and ramp and also fitted are two AN/AAQ-8 infra-red countermeasures pods on the outer wing stations, an AN/AAQ151R detection system, an AN/ALQ-172 detector/jammer, an ALR-69 radar warning receiver, an AN/AAR-44 launch warning receiver with its conical aerial fitted under the fuselage, and the aircraft now has the

Directional Infrared Countermeasures (DIRCM) system installed. All the cockpit and cargo areas have lighting that is compatible with night-vision goggles which are essential for operations."

"The Talon II carries a crew of seven, two fewer than the Talon I, and these comprise a pilot, co-pilot, navigator, flight engineer, electronic warfare officer and two loadmasters. The navigator and EWO's Video Display Terminals (VDTs) give them an unrivalled ability to see the situation and the way ahead. The navigator also controls the FLIR, the ground-mapping radar and the mission management and equipment

For the degree of accuracy called for by its mission, the MC-130 has a dual INS and GPS which will be updated by an AN/ARN-92 LORAN-C

Rolling in low, an MC-130H Combat Talon II

The MC-130 has a 'glass cockpit' cockpit (© Rick Llinares)

status information. The EWO uses his VDTs to display the
electronic warfare data and control all of the passive and active
sensors and jamming equipment. He works very tightly with
the navigator during all phases of a mission. In the cargo hold
we have more modifications, in the shape of the HSLLADS
High-Speed Low-Level Aerial Delivery System. The rear ramp
has been altered and the cargo floor strengthened to allow
22,000lb of cargo to be dropped from the aircraft while it
maintains a 'normal' speed of 250kt at a height of 250ft,
without the need for slowing or climbing - thus preventing the
enemy from finding the exact location of the drop. The
loadmasters rig palletized cargo 'bundles' which are slung out
of the aircraft along rails in the deck floor and ramp. This
method negates the effects of wind and ensures a direct
trajectory to the target. The MC-130's computer system
calculates all the drop parameters using the INS and GPS to
come up with the necessary accurate co-ordinates. We also have

A good underside view is
afforded here

A brace of MC-130s in
nocturnal mode, firing off
flares for effect!

the refuelling capability of the Combat Shadow."

"Once we have our tasking we put together a team of users for the flight, and nothing, but nothing is left to chance. Once we are happy with the schedule we order up some tanker support to give us the 'legs' for the trip; one or two prods might be in order, dependent on where we will be going. Thirty minutes before take-off, the engines and electrics are fired up to give our complex systems a thorough check-out. As you could imagine, there is a high level of 'challenge and response' flying around the cockpit. Once airborne and route-established, we would pick up our first refuel, usually from a KC-10 or KC-135 out over the sea. Once tanked up, we position for the low-level phase, aiming for a coastal penetration at 100 feet. Using the ground-mapping radar, the navigator picks out our minimum threat ingress, and maybe we would put in a feint and move further up the coast before turning back to our original heading. We favour poor/overcast conditions and mountainous terrain to mask our approach to the target and by now as a pilot I am paying very close attention to my 890 line VDTs. Displayed is the T/F radar's 'cue' or 'bug'; this is a circle cut through which a horizontal line is set, giving me the attitude relevant to the terrain. Having already set the 'clearance plane' above the ground, I then follow the 'bug',

making aggressive inputs to the controls to make sure we don't hit anything."

"Also displayed on the VDTs is the FLIR's image, along with temperatures, pressures, altitude, weights and engine performance. The T/F radar also works in turns: it 'looks around corners' at the terrain ahead, which is comforting when

Down low in the valleys – the MC-130 plies its trade

The nose profile of the MC-130E (© Rick Llinares)

A Combat Talon I taxies out
(© Rick Llinares)

Superb artwork! *(© Rick Llinares)*

Night-vision goggles are an essential for 'Talon' operations *(© Rick Llinares)*

we are flying down valleys with only 132ft clearance (the wing span of the MC-130) to play with. With the pilot totally committed to his 'zone of flight', it can get pretty interesting seeing features whizzing past the windows above our heads, especially through the green world of the NVG's. The navigator is now in control of the show, and he is taking constant updates from the INS and GPS, and his route symbology is showing him exactly where we are in relation to the target - and he ensures the system remains 'tight'. Because of the high degree of automation, he does not have to rely on the traditional briefcase full of maps and charts."

"The navigator and the EWO's VDTs give them an unmatched ability to see the situation and are able to present additional FLIR, navigation or EW scenarios to the pilot as they arise. As we approach the target zone, the loadmaster will prepare the back end and, at the signal, the cargo will be offloaded."

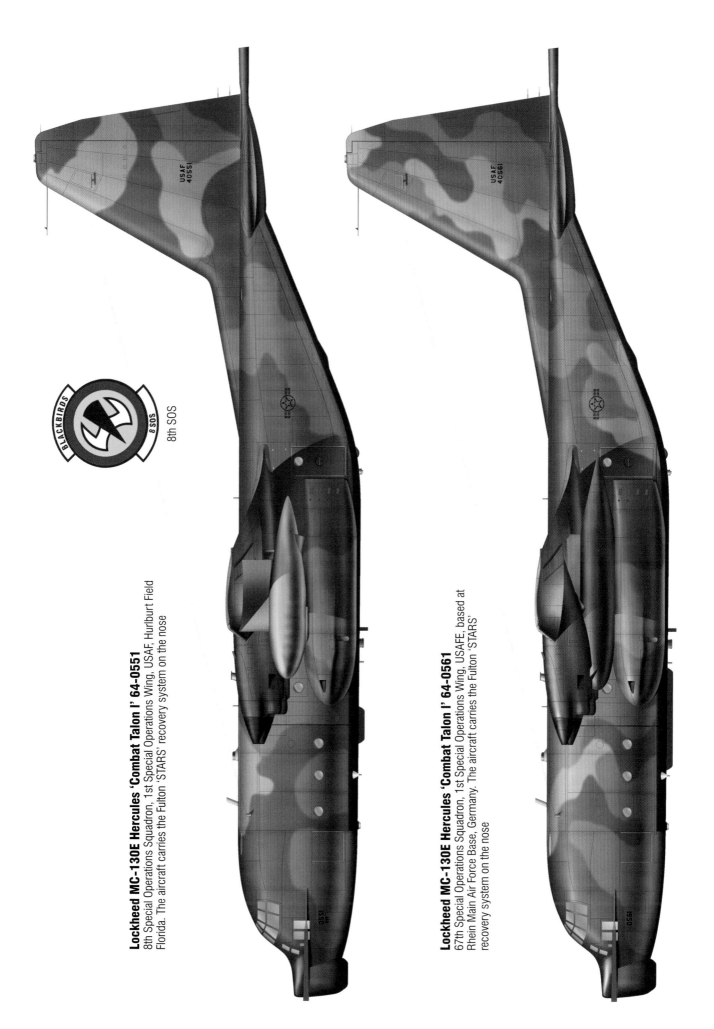

Lockheed MC-130E Hercules 'Combat Talon I' 64-0551
8th Special Operations Squadron, 1st Special Operations Wing, USAF, Hurlburt Field Florida. The aircraft carries the Fulton 'STARS' recovery system on the nose

8th SOS

Lockheed MC-130E Hercules 'Combat Talon I' 64-0561
67th Special Operations Squadron, 1st Special Operations Wing, USAF, USAFE, based at Rhein Main Air Force Base, Germany. The aircraft carries the Fulton 'STARS' recovery system on the nose

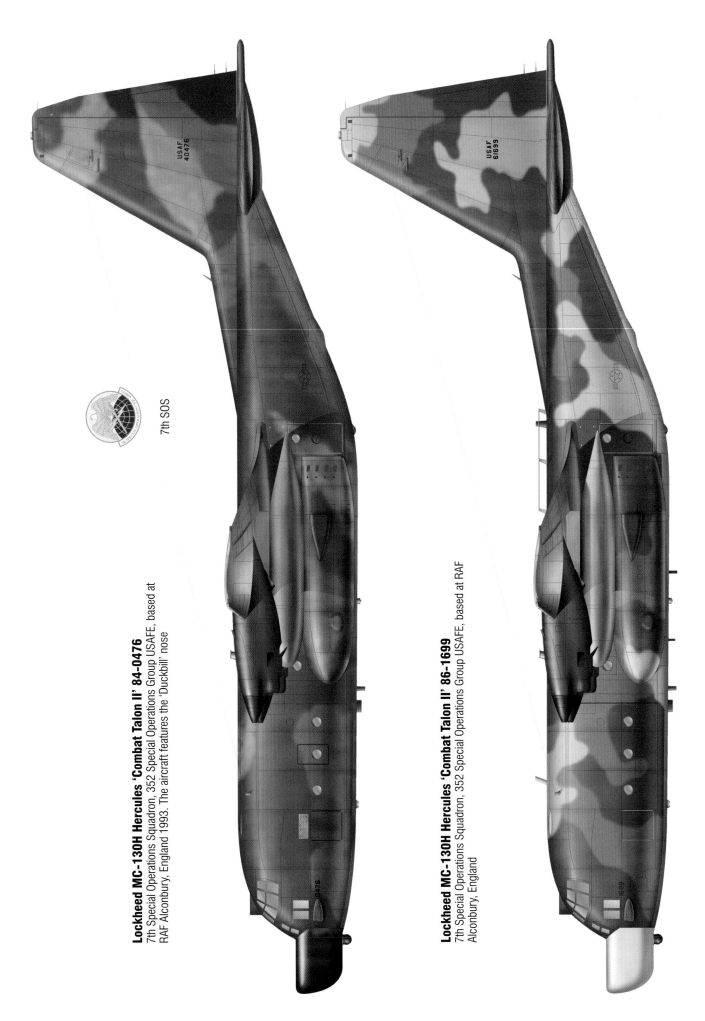

Lockheed MC-130H Hercules 'Combat Talon II' 84-0476
7th Special Operations Squadron, 352 Special Operations Group USAFE, based at RAF Alconbury, England 1993. The aircraft features the 'Duckbill' nose

7th SOS

Lockheed MC-130H Hercules 'Combat Talon II' 86-1699
7th Special Operations Squadron, 352 Special Operations Group USAFE, based at RAF Alconbury, England

USAF 40476

USAF 61699

auletta.it

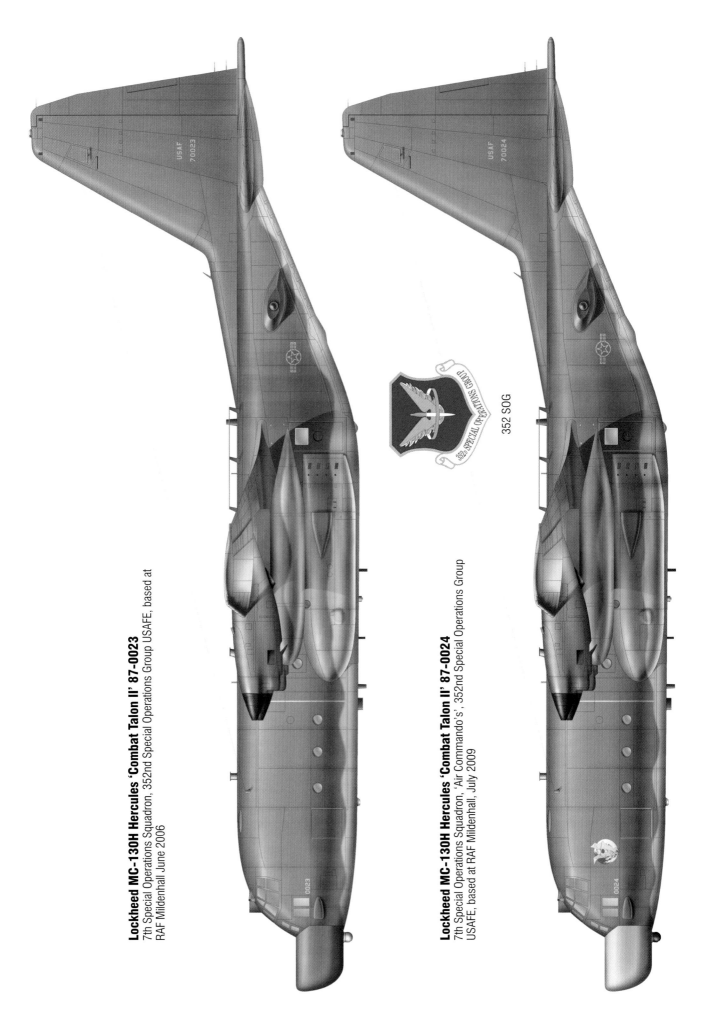

Lockheed MC-130H Hercules 'Combat Talon II' 87-0023
7th Special Operations Squadron, 352nd Special Operations Group USAFE, based at RAF Mildenhall June 2006

Lockheed MC-130H Hercules 'Combat Talon II' 87-0024
7th Special Operations Squadron, 'Air Commando's', 352nd Special Operations Group USAFE, based at RAF Mildenhall, July 2009

352 SOG

The MC-130 Combat Talon
Walkaround

Port side of the 'Duckbill' radome of the MC-130H

Head-on 'Duckbill'

Head on 'ex-Fulton'

Starboard side of the 'ex-Fulton' radome of the MC-130E

Port side of the 'ex-Fulton' radome of the MC-130E

Chaff and flare dispenser fitted to the rear face of the underwing pylon

Extended wing flap

The AN/AAR-44 launch warning receiver with its conical aerial fitted under the fuselage

Starboard side of the 'Duckbill' radome of the MC-130H

Cockpit glazing and appendages

Allison engine

View inside the wing with the flap extended

Side-on view of an underwing fuel tank

Main wheel detail

Air-refuelling pod

The DIRCM housing with fairing

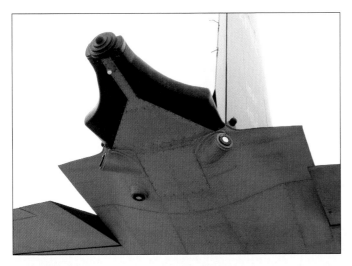

Extreme tail area

Landing light in the wing

Underfuselage antennae

Cargo door area in detail

Underwing fuel tank and pylon

The pilot's office, a mix of old and new displays

The CV-22 Osprey Tilt-Rotor

Chapter 5

Down low, the Osprey is a impressive performer

The Bell-Boeing V-22 Osprey is a multi-mission, military, tilt-rotor aircraft with both a vertical take-off and landing (VTOL) and short take-off and landing (STOL) capability. The Osprey is the world's first production aircraft with one three-bladed prop-rotor, turboprop engine, and transmission nacelle mounted on each wingtip. It is designed to combine the functionality of a conventional helicopter with the long-range, high-speed cruise performance of a turboprop aircraft. For take-off and landing, it typically operates as a helicopter with the nacelles vertical and once airborne, the nacelles rotate forward 90° in as little as twelve seconds for horizontal flight, converting the V-22 to a more fuel-efficient, higher-speed turboprop aircraft. STOL rolling-take-off and landing capability is achieved by having the nacelles tilted forward up to 45°. For compact storage and transport, the V-22's wing rotates to align, front-to-back, with the fuselage. The prop-rotors can also fold in a sequence taking ninety seconds. Developed and manufactured jointly by Bell Helicopter, and Boeing Rotorcraft Systems, it is operated by the United States Marine Corps and Air Force. The failure of the Iran hostage rescue, Operation Eagle Claw in 1980, demonstrated to the United States military a need for a new type of aircraft that could not only take off and land vertically but also could carry combat troops, and do so at speed. The US Department of Defence began the Joint-service Vertical take-off/landing Experimental (JVX) aircraft program in 1981,

Ramp down, the CV-22 shows its abilities

The massive engine nacelles are evident here

With its red instrumentation boom one of the test Ospreys is put through its paces

A brace of AFSOC CV-22 in close formation (© Rick Llinares)

Close-in on the nose section

rolled out in May 1988, and that same year the Army left the program. The first of six MV-22 prototypes first flew on 19 March 1989 in the helicopter mode and on 14 September 1989 as a fixed-wing plane. The third and fourth prototypes successfully completed the Osprey's first Sea Trials on the USS Wasp in December 1990. However, the fourth and fifth prototypes crashed in 1990-91, and flight tests were finally resumed in August 1993 after changes were incorporated in the prototypes. From October 1992 until April 1993, Bell and Boeing redesigned the V-22 to reduce empty weight, simplify manufacture and reduce production costs. This redesigned version became the 'B-model immediate aviation program'.

Kicking up dust as the massive rotor blades bring the Osprey to the hover

firstly under U.S. Army leadership, and then the US Navy/Marine Corps later took the lead, however the JVX combined requirements from the Marine Corps, Air Force, Army and Navy.

The JVX aircraft was designated V-22 Osprey on 15 January 1985 and the USMC variant received the MV-22 designation and the Air Force variant CV-22. This was reversed from normal procedure to prevent Marine Ospreys from having similar designations to aircraft carriers (CV). Full-scale development of the V-22 began in 1986 and the first V-22 was

Extending its IFR probe a CV-22 comes in for some low-level tanking training

A CV-22 in the transition phase between hover and forward flight

A CV-22 fires off decoy flares

The huge rotor blades are clearly seen here

A CV-22 taxies in at the end of another sortie

A pair of CV-22's make a 'pairs landing'

A CV-22 in formation with a Pave Low, the type it has now replaced in AFSOC service *(© Rick Llinares)*

The huge cross section of the Osprey makes it a formidable sight *(© Rick Llinares)*

A pair of Ospreys behind a MC-130P tanker

The Osprey is equipped with a glass cockpit, which incorporates four Multi-Function Displays (MFDs) and one shared Central Display Unit (CDU), allowing the pilots to view a variety of images including: digi-maps centred or decentred on current position, FLIR imagery, primary flight instruments, navigation (TACAN, VOR, ILS, GPS, INS), and system status. The flight director panel of the Cockpit Management System (CMS) allows for fully-coupled autopilot functions which take the aircraft from forward flight into a fifty-foot hover with no pilot interaction other than programming the system. The Osprey is also a fly-by-wire aircraft with triple-redundant flight control systems. With the nacelles pointing straight up in conversion mode at 90° the flight computers command the aircraft to fly like a helicopter, with cyclic forces being applied to a conventional swashplate at the rotor hub. With the nacelles in airplane mode the flaperons, rudder, and elevator fly the aircraft like an airplane. This is a gradual transition which occurs over the entire 96° range of the nacelles. The lower the nacelles, the greater effect of the airplane-mode control

surfaces. The Osprey can be armed with one M240 7.62x51mm NATO or M2 .50 in caliber machine gun pointing rearward that can be fired when the loading ramp is lowered. A GAU-19 three-barrel .50 in Gatling gun can also be mounted below the V-22's nose. BAe Systems has developed a remotely-operated turreted weapons system for the V-22, which was installed on

A pair of Ospreys roll in to land

Special Operations is the most stringent mission of the V-22

The Osprey is also a fly-by-wire aircraft with triple-redundant flight control systems (© Rick Llinares)

An HC-130P trails its hoses for the waiting Ospreys

The US Air Force's first operational deployment of the Osprey sent four CV-22s to Mali in November 2008

Taking on fuel

must be done covertly, at night and in adverse weather. The CV-22 will have enhanced survivability by virtue of the electronic warfare suite specific to the SOF mission as well as meeting the survivability standards identified for the basic MV-22 weapons system. The CV-22 maintains maximum commonality with the MV-22 baseline design. However, several significant differences in equipment tailor the V-22 for the special operations mission. This CV-22 specific equipment includes: a survivor locator system, rope ladders, a low probability of intercept/detection radar altimeter, additional tactical communications, flight engineer seating, a multi-mission tactical terminal (MATT), multi-mode terrain-following/terrain-avoidance radar, aircrew eye and respiratory protection connections, 900 gallons of additional fuel plus cabin auxiliary tanks and computer and digital map upgrade facilities, and a suite of integer-rated radio frequency countermeasures (SIRFC). The CV-22 also has a folding,

half of the first V-22s deployed to Afghanistan in 2009.

The Air Force's first operational CV-22 Osprey was delivered to the 58th Special Operations Wing (58th SOW) at Kirtland Air Force Base, New Mexico on 20 March 2006 to become part of the 58th SOW's fleet of aircraft used for training pilots and crew members for special operations use. Hurlburt Field. The US Air Force's first operational deployment of the Osprey sent four CV-22s to Mali in November 2008 in support of 'Exercise Flintlock' where the CV-22s flew nonstop from Hurlburt Field with in-flight refueling. AFSOC later declared that the 8th Special Operations Squadron reached Initial Operational Capability on 16 March 2009, with six of its planned nine CV-22s operational. In June 2009, CV-22s of the 8th Special Operations Squadron delivered 43,000 pounds of humanitarian supplies to remote villages in Honduras that were not accessible by conventional vehicles, and in November 2009 the 8th SOS Squadron and its six CV-22s returned from a three-month deployment in Iraq.

The Air Force Special Operations Forces/United States Special Operations Command mission is the most stringent mission of the V-22 variants due to the anticipated extended exposure to a high threat environment. The CV-22 variant is slated to travel 500 nautical miles at or below 500 feet, locate a small landing zone, infiltrate and exfiltrate a team of up to eighteen special operations forces, and return to base. This

crashworthy jump-seat with an extended seat pan allowing a flight engineer access to the center and overhead consoles. Also fitted are an AN/AAQ-16B/D FLIR Forward Looking Infra Red pod - facilitating all-weather, day or night flying, an integrated GPS/Inertial navigation systems - allows for highly accurate navigation, an AN/ALQ-211 radar warning receiver and integrated radar jamming system, an AAQ-24 Directed Infrared Countermeasures (DIRCM) system and an AN/ALE-47 Chaff/Flare Dispenser. The Osprey has now replaced the MH-53 Pave Low in Special Operations service.

A pair of CV-22s and a lone MH-53 (© Rick Llinares)

Head-on Osprey! *(© Rick Llinares)*

With the nacelles in airplane mode the flaperons, rudder, and elevator fly the aircraft like an airplane *(© Rick Llinares)*

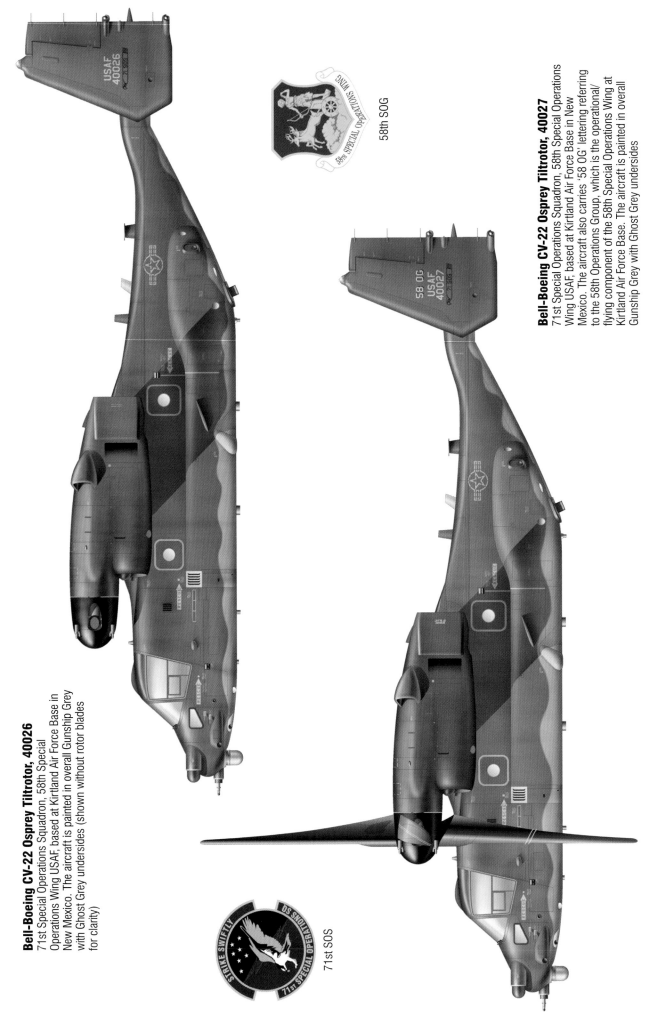

Bell-Boeing CV-22 Osprey Tiltrotor, 40026
71st Special Operations Squadron, 58th Special Operations Wing USAF, based at Kirtland Air Force Base in New Mexico. The aircraft is painted in overall Gunship Grey with Ghost Grey undersides (shown without rotor blades for clarity)

58th SOG

71st SOS

Bell-Boeing CV-22 Osprey Tiltrotor, 40027
71st Special Operations Squadron, 58th Special Operations Wing USAF, based at Kirtland Air Force Base in New Mexico. The aircraft also carries '58 OG' lettering referring to the 58th Operations Group, which is the operational/flying component of the 58th Special Operations Wing at Kirtland Air Force Base. The aircraft is painted in overall Gunship Grey with Ghost Grey undersides

auletta.it

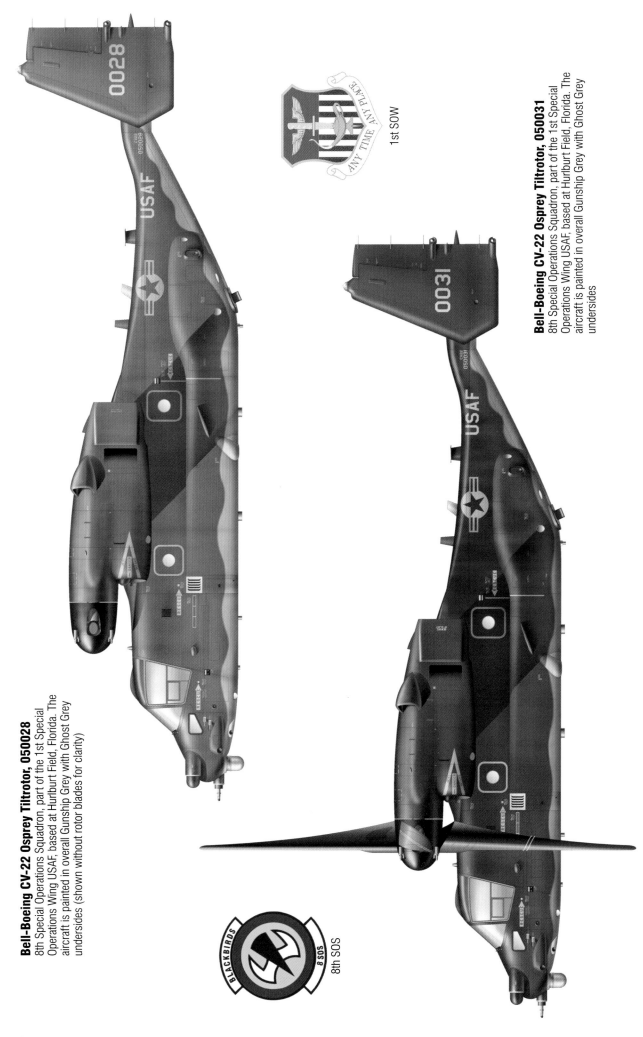

Bell-Boeing CV-22 Osprey Tiltrotor, 050028
8th Special Operations Squadron, part of the 1st Special
Operations Wing USAF, based at Hurlburt Field, Florida. The
aircraft is painted in overall Gunship Grey with Ghost Grey
undersides (shown without rotor blades for clarity)

Bell-Boeing CV-22 Osprey Tiltrotor, 050031
8th Special Operations Squadron, part of the 1st Special
Operations Wing USAF, based at Hurlburt Field, Florida. The
aircraft is painted in overall Gunship Grey with Ghost Grey
undersides

1st SOW

8th SOS

CV-22 Osprey
Walkaround

The CV-22 Osprey (© Rick Llinares)

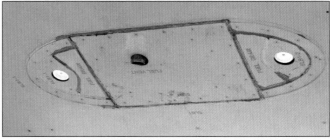

Fuel vent/drain panel

Nose section showing the IFR probe, FLIR turret and radar

Underneath the wing

Looking at the inner face of the engine nacelle

An upward view at the contours of the engine nacelle

Windscreen and forward fuselage side

Note the small fairing on the top of the fuselage

Stencil markings on the forward fuselage

The wing 'root', where the whole assembly can hinge though ninety degrees for storage

Rear fuselage and wheel assembly

Mid-fuselage

Twin tails in detail

Looking up under the wing

Rear aspect showing ramp and ECM gear

A good view of the open engine access panels *(© Rick Llinares)*

Wing flap and grille

The retracted IFR probe and front wheels *(© Rick Llinares)*

Centre console *(© Rick Llinares)*

The underwing nacelle join

With the wing section rotated
a technician checks the
systems *(© Rick Llinares)*

The cockpit instrument panel
(© Rick Llinares)

The MC-130P Combat Shadow

The success of many of the missions undertaken by the US Air Forces Special Operations Command depends on the ability to extend the range or loiter time of its helicopter forces. By definition, a mission brief will see them operating in sensitive areas or behind enemy lines, and these clandestine operations call for a specialised type of airborne tanker. To fulfill this need, once again a modified version of the ubiquitous Hercules was brought into service, the MC-130N/P Combat Shadow. The MC-130P (formerly the HC-130P/N) Combat Shadow flies clandestine or low-visibility, low-level missions into politically sensitive or hostile territory to provide air-refuelling for special operations helicopters. Secondary mission capabilities include airdrop of small special operations teams, small bundles, and zodiac and combat rubber raiding craft, as well as night-vision goggle take-offs and landings, tactical airborne radar approaches and in-flight refuelling as a receiver.

MC-130P's were previously designated HC-130N/P, however,

the 'H' designation is a rescue and recovery mission code and not representative of the aircraft's special operations role, so in February 1996, AFSOC's tanker fleet was redesignated as MC-130Ps, aligning the Combat Shadow with other M-series special operations mission aircraft. MC-130 Combat Shadow and MC-130 Combat Talon aircraft have similar missions, but the Combat Talon has more sophisticated instruments designed for covert operations. However, both aircraft fly infiltration/exfiltration missions – airdrop or land personnel and equipment in hostile territory. The Combat Talon, however, has an electronic countermeasures suite and terrain-following radar that enables it to fly extremely low, counter enemy radar and penetrate deep into hostile territory. Special operations forces improvements have been made to the MC-130P, with modifications including

A Mildenhall based Combat Shadow tucks up its wheels and heads out

Note the overall natural metal finish and the Fulton STARS nose

The MC-130P with the original 'Pinocchio' nose and new **FLIR** *(© Rick Llinares)*

Starboard side refuelling pod

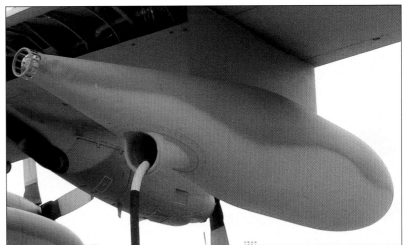

Port side refuelling pod

below: Refuelling a desert camouflaged 'Pave Hawk'

One of the MC-130s with the Fulton nose

improved navigation, communications, threat detection and countermeasures systems. The fully modified Combat Shadow now has a fully integrated inertial navigation and global positioning system, and night-vision goggle-compatible interior and exterior lighting. It also has forward-looking infra-red, missile and radar warning receivers, chaff and flare dispensers and night-vision goggle compatible head-up display. In addition, it has satellite and data burst communications, as well as in-flight refuelling capability as a receiver.

Originally ordered in 1963 and first flown in 1964, the HC-130s

have served in many roles and missions, and the aircraft was initially modified to conduct search and rescue missions, provide a command and control platform, refuel helicopters and carry supplemental fuel for extending range or air refuelling. In the Vietnam War they were used to refuel Jolly and Super Jolly Green Giant helicopters and, as an airborne command post, to direct rescue efforts. The HC-130P was similar to the older HC-130N, and was easily recognised by its unmistakable, and now removed, dorsal 'hump' containing the unique AN/ARD-17 'Cook Tracker' receivers, originally designed to plot returning space capsules, but were found to be of greater use in the CSAR role picking up faint signals from below. Another distinguishing feature is the low-mounted window each side of the fuselage, in front of the wheel bays. The aircraft have two trailing-hose refuelling pods on their outer wing hardpoints, and self-defence is provided by copious numbers of chaff and flare dispensers fitted to the rear fuselage and to the rear of the inner wing pylons. The upper portion of the cargo ramp was also modified to carry high-power flares for illuminating drop sites at night.

Some aircraft were outfitted with the Fulton Surface-To-Air Recovery System (STAR) system, which has now been removed, leaving two distinct nose shapes available. The Fulton recovery kit was air-dropped to a person needing to be recovered, who then put on the overall-type harness. A large, helium-filled balloon was then used to raise a 450-foot (136.5 meters) nylon lift line. The MC-130P engaged the line with its V-shaped yoke and the individual was reeled on board. Red flags on the lift line guide the pilot during daylight recoveries; lights on the lift line were used for night recoveries. The MC-130P flew towards the lift line at 150 miles per hour; snagged it with scissors-like arms

An 'in-cockpit' view of an MC-130P in formation

The Combat Shadow at low-level

A Combat Shadow takes on gas

A welcome sight to any thirsty helo!

A Combat Shadow on finals

The MC-130P (formerly the HC-130P/N) Combat Shadow flies clandestine or low-visibility, low-level missions into politically sensitive or hostile territory

Looking up underneath the nose of an MC-130P

Prop-vortices are evident here as this ex-Fulton Combat Shadow taxies out

At the rear the loadmaster becomes the pilot's eyes

MC-130 Combat Shadow and MC-130 'Combat Talon' aircraft have similar missions, but the Combat Talon has more sophisticated instruments

One of the distinguishing features of the Combat Shadow is the low-set forward window, held over from its rescue days

Refuelling one of AFSOC's latest acquisitions, the CV-22 Osprey

A 'Pave Hawk' prepares to 'plug-in'

Note the full chaff and flare launchers on the rear fuselage *(© Rick Llinares)*

A 'fish-eye' view of the **Combat Shadow** *(© Rick Llinares)*

Thundering away into the distance... *(© Rick Llinares)*

Head-on MC-130P *(© Rick Llinares)*

A pristine looking Combat Shadow gets airborne *(© Rick Llinares)*

A fine view of a fully upgraded Combat Shadow

Note the FLIR under the nose
(© Rick Llinares)

system, and had been prepared to launch if called upon since the late 1960's. An accident in 1982 was the only fatality in seventeen years of live pick-ups, and this damaged the credibility of the personnel pick-up system within the special operations community. That, along with the increased availability of the long-range air-refuellable MH-53J Pave Low and Pave Hawk helicopters, and tightening budgets, caused AFSOC to deactivate the capability in September 1996. Some MC-130Ps have been modified as dual tanker/transports with NVG HUD, MAWS(IR), FLIR and can drop parachutists freefall and static line from a minimum safe height of 500 feet.

As a Combat Shadow pilot explains "Our primary mission is the aerial refuelling of helicopters, and to infil/exfil into hostile territory to deliver or recover personnel and equipment at low level, and under the cover of darkness We fly anything between 100 and 1,000ft, comm's out, lights out, both internal and external and we regularly practice NVG aided landings and take-offs in complete darkness. We normally pass fuel at around 115 knots, which is really close to our stall speed, and very slow for such a big airplane. Our normal join-up with the helo's means that they like to be on-time/early, whereas we like to be on-time/late at the RV. That gives us time to catch up and overtake them, roll out the hoses and let them plug in. We sometimes had problems meeting up with the Pave Lows; maybe they're late, or not where they said they would be; in these instances we have a number of methods to find them. We can use the TACAN or IFF interrogator, or we can try the C-130's radar, but like other 'slick 130s' it's not designed for air intercept. We try where possible to tank in as low-threat an environment as we can; this gives all parties the best possible chance of survival".

"Once we have picked up our 'trade', we line up about three miles behind them, then at one mile out the flaps are set to 70 per cent and the speed is pegged back to between 115 and 120 knots. As we close, the navigator starts calling off the closure, and as we come abeam, the flight engineer rolls out the hoses. At the rear the loadmaster now becomes the pilot's eyes, giving him constant updates about the helo's progress as they move into pre-contact positions. Once contact is made, a light comes up on the flight engineer's panel and he begins the fuel transfer. We have two methods of refuelling, 'automatic' which means the engineer dials in a set amount and the feed shuts off at that point, or purely 'manual' where the helicopter pilot decides how much he wants to take on board. For a Pave Low the take-on is around 7,000lb of gas, and we have up to 82,500lb to give away when fully loaded. The fuel is carried within the MC-130's own tanks as well as in up to two 11,000lb 'Benson' tanks mounted in the mid-section of the cargo hold."

located on the nose and the person or equipment was lifted off, experiencing less shock than that caused by a parachute opening. Aircrew members then used a hydraulic winch to pull the person or equipment aboard through the open rear cargo door.

Col. Allison Brooks, then Commander of the ARRS, and A3C Ronald Doll participated in the first human testing of the Fulton surface-to-air two-man recovery kit at Edwards AFB, California in May 1966. Recovery kits were designed for one and two-man recoveries, but eventually proved impractical for most rescue purposes. By 1996 the 8th SOS was the only unit in the world that maintained crew proficiency in the use of the Fulton recovery

Trailing hoses, as this MC-130P waits for its 'trade'
(© Rick Llinares)

Trailing heat haze in its wake an MC-130P taxies out
(© Rick Llinares)

Four turning! *(© Rick Llinares)*

A good view of the nose section of the MC-130P
(© Rick Llinares)

A 'receiver's eye view' chasing down an MC-130P
(© Rick Llinares)

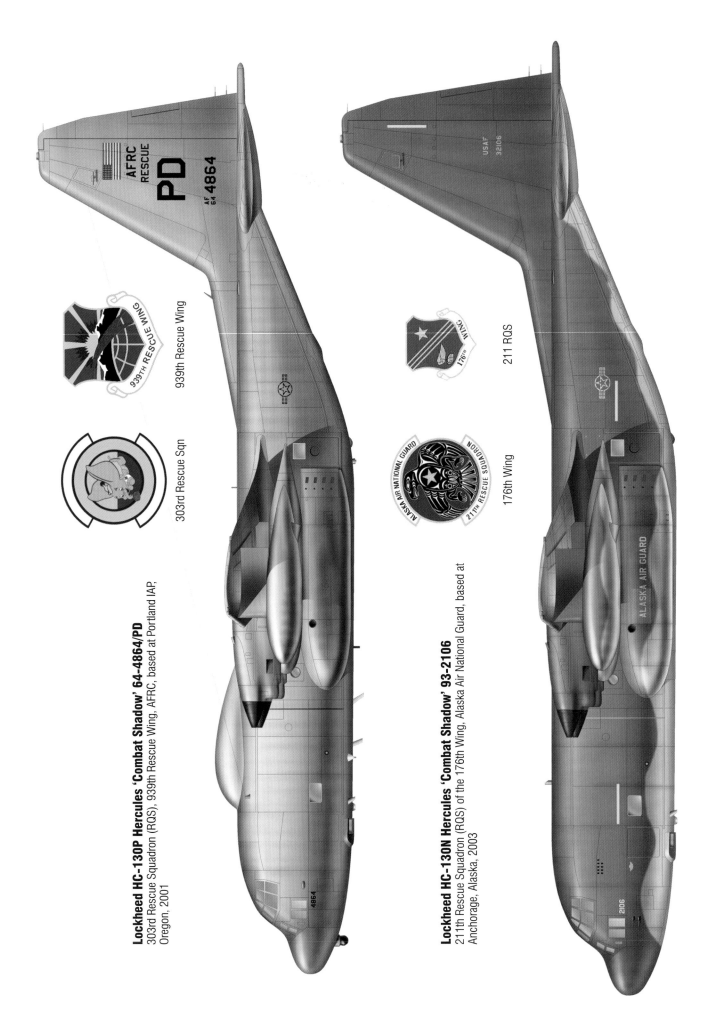

Lockheed HC-130P Hercules 'Combat Shadow' 64-4864/PD
303rd Rescue Squadron (RQS), 939th Rescue Wing, AFRC, based at Portland IAP, Oregon, 2001

939th Rescue Wing

303rd Rescue Sqn

Lockheed HC-130N Hercules 'Combat Shadow' 93-2106
211th Rescue Squadron (RQS) of the 176th Wing, Alaska Air National Guard, based at Anchorage, Alaska, 2003

211 RQS

176th Wing

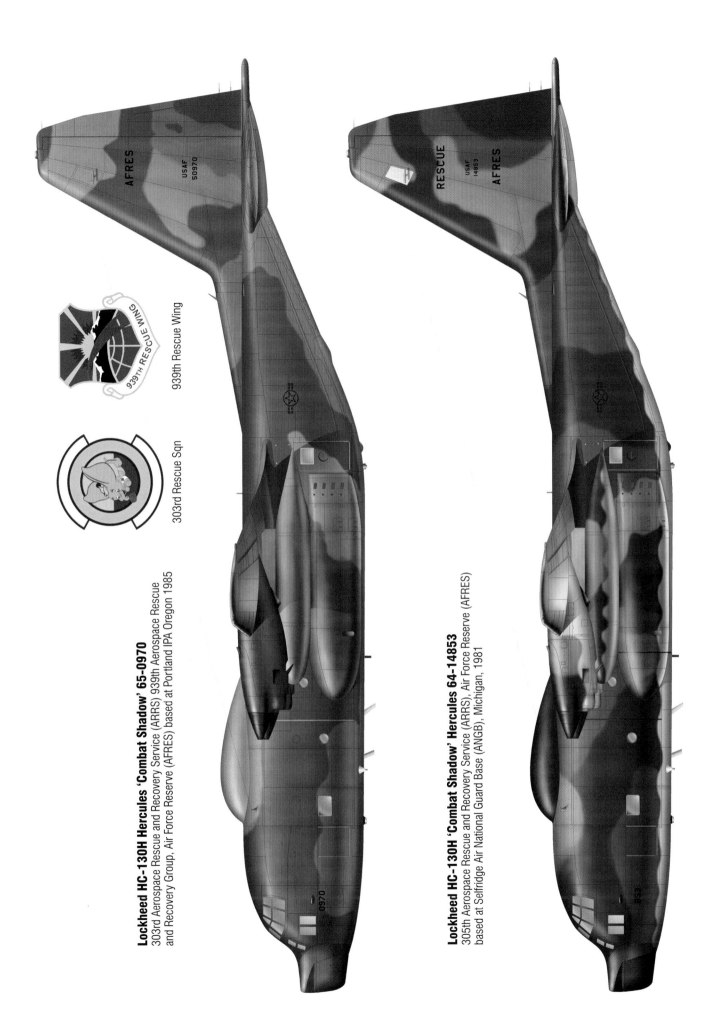

939th Rescue Wing

303rd Rescue Sqn

Lockheed HC-130H Hercules 'Combat Shadow' 65-0970
303rd Aerospace Rescue and Recovery Service (ARRS) 939th Aerospace Rescue and Recovery Group, Air Force Reserve (AFRES) based at Portland IPA Oregon 1985

Lockheed HC-130H 'Combat Shadow' Hercules 64-14853
305th Aerospace Rescue and Recovery Service (ARRS), Air Force Reserve (AFRES) based at Selfridge Air National Guard Base (ANGB), Michigan, 1981

The EC-130 Commando Solo

Chapter 7

An EC-130E 'Rivet Rider'

The EC-130 family are modified versions of the Hercules and include the Commando Solo used to conduct psychological operations (PSYOP) and civil affairs broadcast missions in the standard AM, FM, HF TF channels and military communications bands, the ABCCC 'Airborne Battlefield Command and Control Centre' and the 'Compass Call' used to disrupt enemy communications. Missions are flown at the maximum altitudes possible to ensure optimum propagation patterns, by both day and night, and a typical mission consists of a single-ship orbit which is offset from the desired audience, and 'targets' may be either military or civilian.

A rather weary looking 'Compass Call'

EC-130E ABCCC

The EC-130E ABCCC consisted of seven aircraft that were used as an 'Airborne Battlefield Command and Control Centre', and were flown by the 355th Special Operations Wing at Davis Monthan AFB. The EC-130E was designed to carry the USC-48 Airborne Battlefield Command and Control Center Capsules (ABCCC III) and these one-of-a kind aircraft included the addition of external antennae to accommodate the vast number of radios in the capsule, heat exchanger pods for additional air conditioning, an aerial refuelling system and special mounted rails for uploading and downloading the USC-48 capsule. The ABCCC had distinctive air conditioner intakes forward of the engines, the so-called 'Mickey Mouse ears', two HF radio probes-towards the tips of both wings, and three mushroom-shaped antennae on the top of the aircraft - and of course, numerous antennae on the belly. The ABCCC system was a high-tech automated airborne

Note the 'Mickey Mouse ears' on this EC-130E ABCCC

An EC-130H taking on fuel

command and control facility featuring computer generated color displays, digitally controlled communications, and rapid data retrieval. The platform's twenty-three fully securable radios, secure teletype, and fifteen automatic fully computerised consoles, allowed the battle staff to quickly analyse current combat situations and direct offensive air support towards fast-developing targets. The ABCCC was equipped also with the Joint Tactical Information Distribution System. The flight deck crew was a standard C-130 crew and the airborne battle staff tailored to fit any mission based on operational needs. The battle staff comprised four functional areas: command, operations, intelligence, and communications. Normally it included twelve members, working in nine different specialities including: the Director of Airborne Battle Staff, the Battle Staff Operations Officer, an Airborne Intelligence Officer, an Airborne Intelligence Technician, an Airborne Strike Controller, an Airborne Close Air Support Co-Coordinator, an Airborne Maintenance Technician, an Airborne Systems Communication Operator and a Ground Liaison Officer. In May 2002 the EC-130E missions were transferred to the E-3 AWACS and the E-8 Joint STARS aircraft.

An EC-130 comes in to land

EC-130E Commando Solo/Rivet Rider

The EC-130E Commando Solo (initially known as Volant Solo) is available to commanders for localised targeting of specific avenues of communication. Flown by the 193rd Special Operations Group (ANG) at Harrisburg International Airport, the 'Electrons not Bullets' mission is flown by the EC-130E

An EC-130H 'Compass Call' – note the various appendages!

The rear aspect of the
EC-130J showing the bullet
fairings

An excellent head-on shot of
the EC-130J

EC-130J Cockpit detail

Commando Solo and the EC-130E(RR) 'Rivet Rider' versions.
A multi-purpose asset capable of conducting PSYOP and EW,
the EC-130E, Commando Solo, is an airborne platform
primarily designed for PSYOP and can conduct psychological
broadcast missions in the standard AM, FM, HF, TV and
military communications bands. Highly specialised
modifications have been made to the latest version of the
EC-130E and these include enhanced navigation systems, self-
protection equipment, and the capability of broadcasting
colour television on a multitude of worldwide standards
throughout the TV VHF/UHF ranges. The distinguishing
features of the EC-130E 'Rivet Rider' are one oversized blade
antenna under each wing with a third extending forward from
the vertical fin. A retractable wire antenna is released from the
modified beavertail, with a second extending from the belly
and held vertical by a 500 pound weight. The EC-130E
Commando Solo conducts psychological operations and civil
affairs broadcast missions in the standard AM, FM, HF, TV, and
military communications bands. Modifications on the
Commando Solo EC-130s included the addition of two 6ft
diameter, 23ft long pods mounted under each wing (outboard
of the axe-head antennae), and these house the aerials for high-
frequency colour TV channels. Also prominent are four 'bullet'
fairings protruding from either side of the tail and these are

dedicated to low-frequency TV broadcasting, with the tail-
mounted blade antennae being deleted. Two trailing-wire
aerials can be extended, to provide both HF and AM omni-
directional coverage. Self-protection is also enhanced, with the
addition of IR jammers and chaff and flare dispensers.
Missions begin when a problem area is identified and the
appropriate method of PSYOPS decided upon. This process
starts at the State Department with a Situation Evaluation and
then relevant messages are produced at the Army's 4th
Psychological Operations Group at Fort Bragg. Once these are
approved they are delivered to the 193rd where the Joint Forces

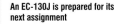

Note the array of antennae at
the rear

An EC-130J is prepared for its
next assignment

medium, high, very high or ultra-high frequencies, or 'audio' positions. The mission compartment has various broadcast sources, transmitters and a 'live' microphone. The mission control chief plans where the EC-130 will orbit in order to hit the target audience with the best possible signal and the EC-130 is able to overpower local transmissions or broadcast on open frequencies. The search operator also monitors the radio and TV frequencies to find one that is clear of other broadcasts and is within the target area. Depending on the frequency, the operators will select either HF/MF or VHF/UHF, and tune up their transmitters inside the aircraft, matching them with the corresponding antennae outside. The signals can then be sent from either side of the aircraft, depending on which direction the target is. One of the operators then selects and plays a message across to the transmitting operators, who broadcast its content over the airways.

EC-130J Commando Solo II

The original EC-130E's were retired in 2006, and their place was taken by the new EC-130Js, with the current mission equipment being moved from the old aircraft to the new models. The EC-130J Commando Solo II, like the EC-130E, is able to conduct airborne radio and color television broadcasting on any frequency and in any format anywhere in the world.

EC-130H Rivet Fire/Compass Call

Compass Call is the designation for thirteen modified versions of the EC-130 configured to perform tactical command, control and communications countermeasures or C3CM and flown by the 41st Electronic Combat Squadron from Davis Monthan AFB. Targeting command and control systems provides commanders with an immense advantage before and during the air campaign and 'Compass Call' provides a non-lethal means of disrupting enemy command and control, degrading his combat capability. Specifically, the modified aircraft uses noise jamming to prevent communication or degrade the transfer of information essential to command and control of weapon systems and other resources. It primarily supports tactical air operations but also can provide jamming support to ground force operations. Modifications to the aircraft include

Command forms a Joint PSYOPS Task Force to evaluate and assign target areas. Once airborne, the mission is coordinated by the five electronic communication system operators and the mission control chief. They are situated in the mission compartment, which is located in the main body of the aircraft. These operators occupy either 'search' positions, covering

EC-130 COMPASS CALL	
Electronic warfare, suppression of enemy air defenses and offensive counter information	
Power Plant:	Four Allison T56-A-15 turboprops
Thrust:	4,591 prop shaft horsepower
Wingspan:	132 feet, 7 inches (39.7 metres)
Length:	97 feet, 9 inches (29.3 metres)
Height:	38 feet, 3 inches (11.4 metres)
Weight:	101,000 pounds (45,813 kilograms)
Max Take-off Weight:	155,000 pounds (69,750 kilograms)
Fuel capacity:	62,000 pounds (28,182 kilograms)
Speed:	300 mph
Range:	2,295 miles (3,694 kilometres)
Ceiling:	25,000 feet (7.6 kilometres)
Armament:	Non-kinetic energy waveforms
Crew:	Thirteen (two pilots, navigator, flight engineer, two electronic warfare officers, mission crew supervisor, four crypto logic linguists, acquisition operator and an airborne maintenance technician)

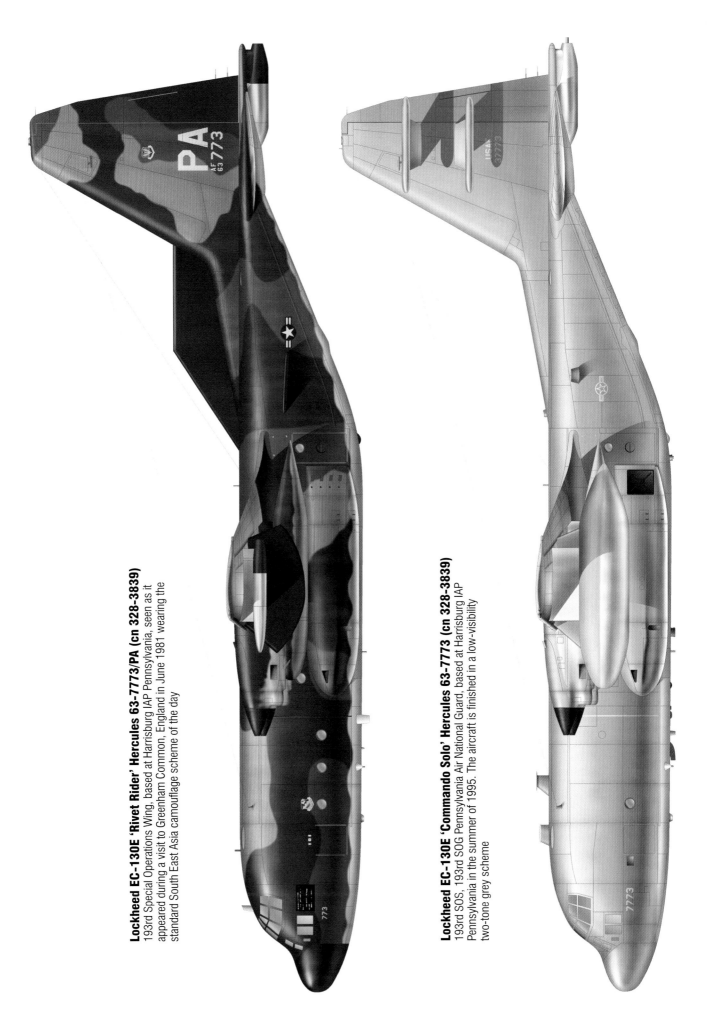

Lockheed EC-130E 'Rivet Rider' Hercules 63-7773/PA (cn 328-3839)
193rd Special Operations Wing, based at Harrisburg IAP Pennsylvania, seen as it appeared during a visit to Greenham Common, England in June 1981 wearing the standard South East Asia camouflage scheme of the day

Lockheed EC-130E 'Commando Solo' Hercules 63-7773 (cn 328-3839)
193rd SOS, 193rd SOG Pennsylvania Air National Guard, based at Harrisburg IAP Pennsylvania in the summer of 1995. The aircraft is finished in a low-visibility two-tone grey scheme

Note the 'axe-head' wing
antennae and the enlarged fin
on this EC-130E(RR)

an electronic countermeasures system (Rivet Fire), air-refuelling capability and associated navigation and communications systems. During Operation Desert Storm EC-130H Compass Call electronic warfare aircraft, operating outside Iraqi airspace, jammed communications, hindering the effectiveness of Iraq's integrated air defence network. The EC-130H aircraft carries a combat crew of thirteen people. Four are responsible for aircraft flight and navigation, while nine members operate and maintain the Rivet Fire equipment. The mission crew consists of an electronic warfare officer, who is the mission crew commander (MCC), an experienced cryptologist/linguist, an Acquisition Operator, a High Band Operator, four analysis operators, and an airborne maintenance technician (Either the Analysis Operator or the High Band Operator can be promoted to the position of mission crew supervisor (MCS). Aided by the automated system, the crew analyses the signal environment, designate targets and ensures the system is operating effectively.

An EC-130E 'Rivet Rider' in an early camouflage incarnation

The busy interior of the
Commando Solo

The EC-130
Walkaround

Inside the communications centre

Close-up on the EC-130J engines

Close-up on the tail of an EC-130J showing the trailing aerial fairing

Infra-Red Countermeasures system

Close-in on the bullet fairings on the tail of an EC-130J

The MC-130W Combat Spear

The MC-130W Combat Spear was developed to supplement the MC-130 Combat Talon and Combat Shadow forces as an interim measure after several training accidents and contingency losses in supporting the Global War on Terrorism. The Combat Spear program modified twelve C-130H-2 airframes from the 1987-1990 production run, acquired from airlift units in the Air Force Reserve Command and Air National Guard, and the use of the H-2 airframes allowed the installation of SOF systems already configured for Combat Talons without expensive and

73rd SOS badge

time-consuming development that would be required of new production C-130J aircraft. The Combat Spears however, do not have the terrain-following/terrain-avoidance capability of the more complex Combat Talon. The MC-130Ws are assigned to the 73rd Special Operations Squadron at Cannon Air Force Base, New Mexico. Initially nicknamed the 'Whiskey' the MC-130W was officially dubbed the Combat Spear in May 2007 to honour the historical legacy of the Combat Talons in Vietnam, however the MC-130W is also unofficially known as the 'Combat Wombat'

A standard system of special forces avionics equips the MC-130W: a fully integrated Global Positioning System and Inertial Navigation System; a AN/APN-241 Low Power Colour weather/navigation radar; interior and exterior NVG-compatible lighting; advanced threat detection and automated countermeasures, including an AN/AAQ-17 active infra-red countermeasures as well as chaff and flares; upgraded communication suites, including include dual satellite communications using data burst transmission to make track-back difficult; aerial refuelling capability; and the ability to act as an aerial tanker for helicopters and CV-22 Osprey aircraft using Mk.32B-902E refuelling pods. Structural improvements to the basic C-130H also include the addition of the Universal Aerial Refuelling Receptacle Slipway Installation (UARRSI), and a strengthened empennage. The UARRSI allows the aircraft to

Aerial refuelling a pair of Pave Low helicopters

The MC-130W was designed to take the weight from the over-tasked Combat Talon

The MC-130W is a modified C-130H-2 airframe

High Speed Low Level Aerial Delivery System (HSLLADS) floor

An MC-130W taxies in, note the shape of the Mk.32B-902E refuelling pods

conduct in-flight refuelling as a receiver, and strengthening of the tail will allow High Speed Low Level Aerial Delivery System (HSLLADS) airdrop operations.

In May 2009, following a lapse of plans to acquire and develop an AC-27J 'gunship light' to replace the aging, operations-stressed AC-130 inventory, the Air Force began exploring an option of converting MC-130Ws into interim gunships. In addition to employing wing-mounted Hellfire/DAGR missiles, the 'Combat Spears' would be convertible by the use of roll-on, roll-off kits featuring a Bushmaster II Mk44 30mm gun, sensors, communications systems and precision-guided munitions attachable to permanent installations in the aircraft, known as the Adaptive Carriage Environment (ACE). The PGMs would be in the form of the 'Gunslinger' weapons system, a launch tube designed to deploy up to ten stand-off GBU-44/B 'Viper Strikes' or similar small stand-off munitions in quick succession.

Combat Spears do not have a terrain-following/terrain-avoidance capability of the more complex Combat Talon

The MH/HH-60G
Pave Hawk

Chapter 9

Hoisting from the hover

A lthough no longer in the direct Special Operations Command inventory, the 'Pave Hawk' has been, and continues to be at the forefront of Combat Search and Rescue, and covert infiltration and exfiltration of combat equipped personnel, and therefore warrants a place in this book. The MH-60G/HH-60G Pave Hawk is a twin-engined medium-lift helicopter with the capability of independent rescue operations in combat areas up to and including medium-threat environments. Recoveries are made by landing or by alternate means, such as rope ladder or hoist, and the aircraft use low-level tactical flight profiles to avoid threats and the crews utilise NVG's, and the aircraft's radar and FLIR for

night operations. The basic crew normally consists of five: pilot, co-pilot, flight engineer, and two Para Rescuemen (PJs).

Based on the proven UH-60 Blackhawk helicopter the MH/HH-60 has sliding doors on each side of the troop and cargo compartment to allow rapid loading and unloading of troops or material and is equipped with a rescue hoist with a 200-foot cable with a 600-pound lift capacity. The hoist can recover a Stokes litter patient or three people simultaneously on a forest penetrator, and the aircraft also has provisions for an external stores support system, and all Pave Hawks have an automatic flight control system to stabilise the aircraft in typical flight altitudes. The helicopter has limited self-protection, which is provided by two 7.62mm mini-guns mounted in the cabin window and two .50 calibre machine guns which can also be mounted in the rear cabin doors. The

A pair of 'Pave Hawks' fast-rope troops, kicking up dust in the process

Wearing their original green and grey scheme, a pair of 'Pave Hawks' prepare to take on fuel

Having deposited its 'charges' the 'Pave Hawk' moves off

The hoist can recover a Stokes litter patient

A skid-equipped 'Pave Hawk' from Alaska fast-roping troops

Kicking up some dust as a 'Pave Hawk' prepares to deposit its troops

guns on the Pave Hawk are mounted externally, instead of being hinged to swing inside the cabin to lock in place. This provides flight engineers, who operate the aircraft's weapons, with the advantage of closing the gunner's windows when flying in sub-zero temperatures, and this also frees up cabin space. They are also equipped with Bendix colour all-weather radar, an APR-39A(V)1 radar warning receiver, ALQ-144A infrared jammer, Hover Infrared Suppression System (HIRSS), M-130 chaff dispenser, and precision navigation equipment in

The 'Pave Hawk' is a twin-engined medium-lift helicopter

SPIE rigging into the landing zone (© Rick Llinares)

the shape of GPS, INS and Doppler all afford additional threat avoidance and protection. The helicopter has a maximum speed of 193 knots with a cruise speed of 120 to 140 knots and an unrefuelled range of 480 nautical miles, and in-flight refuelling greatly extends this range so Pave Hawks are equipped with a retractable IFR probe and internal auxiliary fuel tanks.

The mission systems on the Pave Hawk make it ideally suited for operations with special warfare units. Combat-equipped personnel can be covertly inserted and/or extracted in any

The mission systems on the 'Pave Hawk' make it ideally suited for operations with special warfare units

A pilot's eye view of the tanking procedure

A great view of the external guns and shell collector tubes here

Troops using a rope ladder

Gunners on the look-out!

A good underside view of the cab area is afforded here

Combat-equipped personnel can be covertly inserted and/or extracted in any terrain with precise GPS navigation accuracy

A Pave Hawk 'gasses-up'
(© Rick Llinares)

A casualty is loaded on board

Preparing to 'prod'
(© Rick Llinares)

Blades kicking up blades!
(© Rick Llinares)

Getting ready for engine start
(© Rick Llinares)

A brace of Pave Hawks coming in low (© Rick Llinares)

On the ground the Pararescueman surveys the area (© Rick Llinares)

terrain with precise GPS navigation accuracy. A variety of insertion and extraction techniques are available, including landing, hoisting, fast-rope, rappel, paradrop, McGuire or SPIE Rig, and CRRC. Additionally, Helicopter Visit Board Search and Seizure (HVBSS) operations may be conducted using one or more of these insertion/extraction techniques. HVBSS missions are designed to take control of a ship considered to be a Contact of Interest (COI). The ability to interdict or 'take down' shipping during enforcement of a naval blockade requires precise planning and execution. Tethered Duck (T-Duck) was implemented to rapidly insert troops and a Combat Rubber Raiding Craft (CRRC) to water areas. The troops then fast-rope down to the CRRC after it is lowered into the water, and the motor is then hoisted down to complete the procedure. Parachute operations are used for inserting troops when the

The Pave Hawk can be armed with a 7.62mm mini-gun (© Rick Llinares)

helicopters are unable to land with a minimum free-fall drop altitude of 2,500 feet AGL. As of 2002 there were no MH/HH-60s in special operations use, with the last user being 55th Special Operations Squadron at Hurlburt Field. Interestingly, in a CASR mission, the HH-60 rescue helicopters retained their Vietnam ''Jolly' callsign, the 'Sandy' role now being performed by A-10 or F-16 jets.

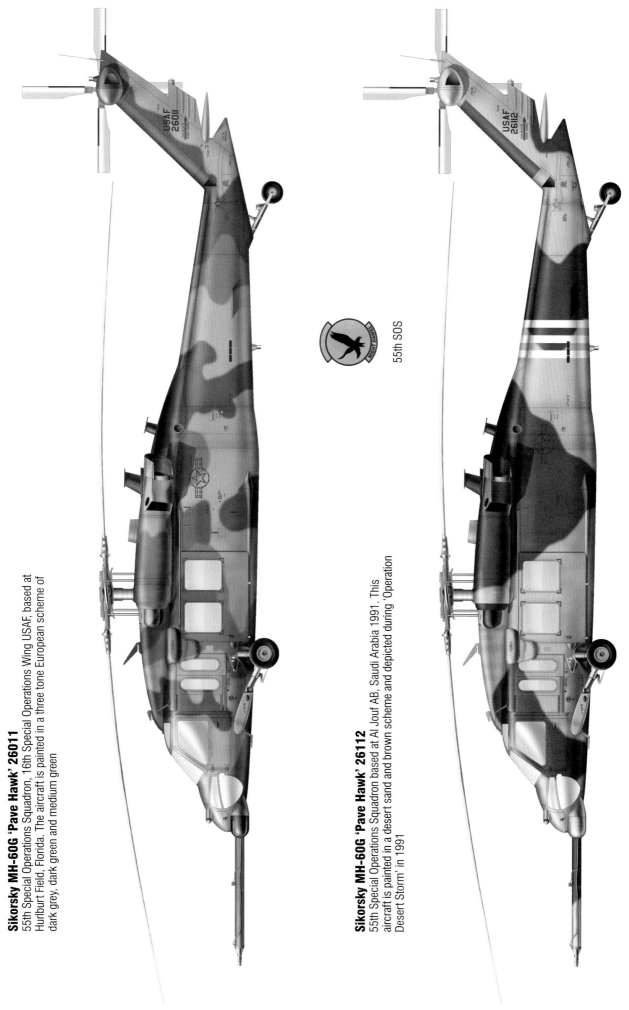

Sikorsky MH-60G 'Pave Hawk' 26011
55th Special Operations Squadron, 16th Special Operations Wing USAF, based at
Hurlburt Field, Florida. The aircraft is painted in a three tone European scheme of
dark grey, dark green and medium green

Sikorsky MH-60G 'Pave Hawk' 26112
55th Special Operations Squadron based at Al Jouf AB, Saudi Arabia 1991. This
aircraft is painted in a desert sand and brown scheme and depicted during 'Operation
Desert Storm' in 1991

55th SOS

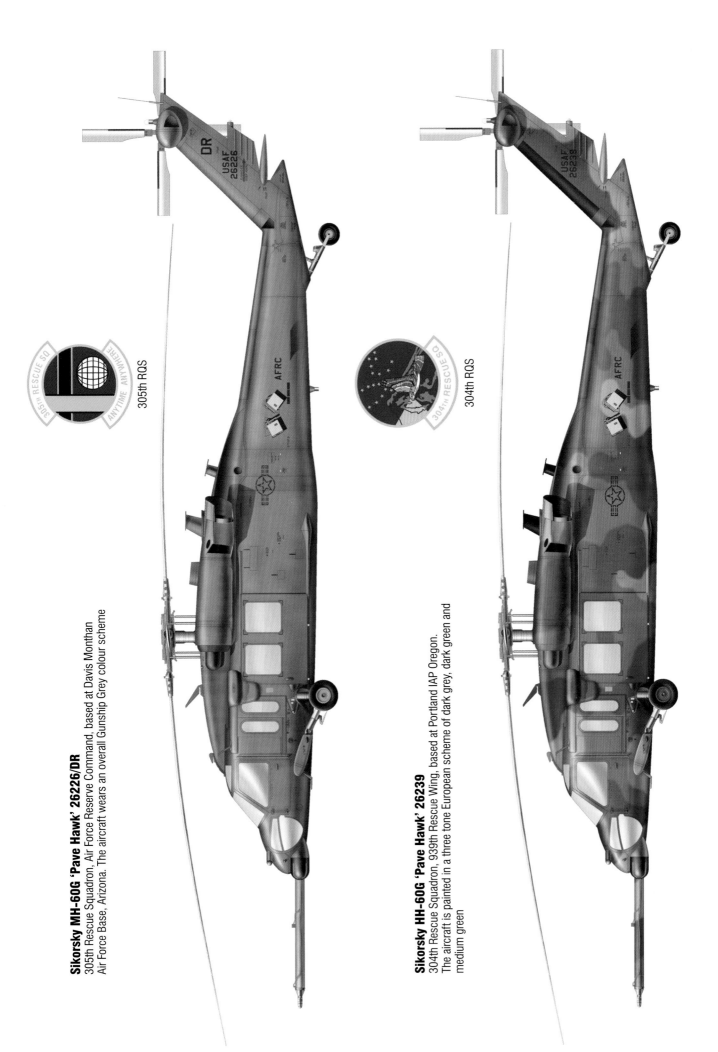

Sikorsky MH-60G 'Pave Hawk' 26226/DR
305th Rescue Squadron, Air Force Reserve Command, based at Davis Monthan
Air Force Base, Arizona. The aircraft wears an overall Gunship Grey colour scheme

305th RQS

Sikorsky HH-60G 'Pave Hawk' 26239
304th Rescue Squadron, 939th Rescue Wing, based at Portland IAP Oregon.
The aircraft is painted in a three tone European scheme of dark grey, dark green and
medium green

304th RQS

MH/HH-60G Pave Hawk
Walkaround

Bendix radar

A head-on view of the Pave Hawk *(© Rick Llinares)*

One of the two .50 calibre machine guns carried by the Pave Hawk *(© Rick Llinares)*

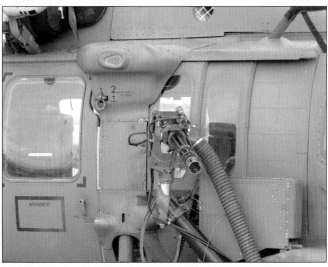

One of the 7.62 mini-guns *(© Rick Llinares)*

Close-in on the IFR probe

Tail area in detail *(© Rick Llinares)*

Engine cowling detail

Sliding rear cargo door

Wheel detail and support, and of course the 7.62mm mini-gun!
(© Rick Llinares)

Part of the HIRSS Hover Infra-Red Suppression System

Rear EMC boxes

Note the deflected tailplane here

The tailboom folds for storage

Glossary of Terms

ABCCC .... Airborne Battlefield Command and Control Centre
AFB .... Air Force Base
AFRES .... Air Force Reserve
AFSOC .... Air Force Special Operations Command
ALLTV .... All Light Level Television
APS .... Armour Protection System
ARRS .... Aerospace Rescue And Recovery
CCIP .... Constantly Computed Impact Point
CCTS .... Combat Crew Training Squadron
CDU .... Central Display Unit
CIA .... Central Intelligence Agency
DIRCM .... Directional Infrared Countermeasures
DTA .... Dual Target Attack
ECM .... Electronic Counter Measures
EIRS .... Engine Infrared Suppression
EWO .... Electronic Warfare Officer
FID .... Foreign Internal Defence
FLIR .... Forward looking Infra-Red
HIRSS .... Hover Infra-red Suppression System
HSLLADS ..... High Speed Low Level Aerial Delivery System
HVBSS .... Helicopter Visit Board Search and Seizure
IDAS/MATT .... Defensive Avionics System/Multi-Mission Advanced Tactical Terminal
IDS .... Infrared Detection Set

LLLTV .... Low Light Level Television
MFD .... Multi-Function Display
MTI .... Moving Target Indicator
NVG .... Night Vision Goggles
SINCGARS ..... Single Channel Ground and Air Radio System
SIRFC .... Suite of Integer-rated Radio Frequency Countermeasures
SLAB .... Sideways Looking Airborne Radar
SOG .... Special Operations Group
SOLL .... Special Operations Low Level
SOS .... Special Operations Squadron
SOW .... Special Operations Wing
STARS .... Surface-To-Air Recovery System
STOL .... Short Take-Off and Landing
TACAN .... Tactical Air Navigation
TF/TA .... Terrain Following/Terrain Avoidance
UARRSI .... Universal Aerial Refueling Receptacle Slipway Installation
USAFSOF ...... USAF Special Operations Force
VDT .... Video Display Terminal
VTOL .... Vertical Take-Off and Landing

Inside a MH/HH-60G Pave Hawk

The XFC-130H

Downward-firing rockets slow the Hercules

Credible Sport

Operation 'Credible Sport' was an audacious plan to launch a second rescue attempt in order to recover the US hostages from the American Embassy in Iran. The 'Credible Sport' program was a developmental project to create capabilities for a 'Super STOL' aircraft after the dramatic failure of Operation 'Eagle Claw'. The 'Credible Sport' concept called for modified C-130 Hercules cargo planes to land in the Amjadien Soccer Stadium across the street from the American Embassy in Tehran and airlift out the rescued hostages. The aircraft would then be flown to, and landed on an aircraft carrier for immediate medical treatment of injured hostages. Three MC-130 Combat Talon crews – all 'Eagle Claw' veterans – were assigned to fly the three aircraft, all drawn from the 463rd Military Airlift Wing.

The three C-130s were modified under a top secret project at Eglin Air Force Base, Florida and this called for two to be customised to the proposed XFC-130H configuration, and the third to be used as a test bed for various rocket packages blistered onto the forward and aft fuselage, which would theoretically enable the aircraft to land and take-off within

MK-56 rockets taken from the US Navy's RIM-66 Standard Missile, mounted on the lower rear fuselage for take-off assist, two Shrikes mounted in pairs on wing pylons to correct yaw during take-off transition, and two 'ASROCs' mounted at the rear of the tail to prevent it from striking the ground from over-rotation. Other STOL features included a

Lockheed YMC-130H Hercules Modifications
Note: Modified flaps not shown

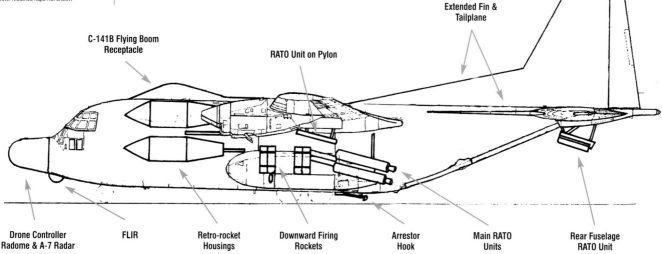

Extended Fin & Tailplane

C-141B Flying Boom Receptacle

RATO Unit on Pylon

Drone Controller Radome & A-7 Radar | **FLIR** | **Retro-rocket Housings** | **Downward Firing Rockets** | **Arrestor Hook** | **Main RATO Units** | **Rear Fuselage RATO Unit**

the confines of the sports arena. The XFC-130H aircraft were modified by the installation of thirty rockets in multiple sets: eight forward-pointed 'ASROC' rocket motors mounted around the forward fuselage to stop the aircraft, eight downward-pointed 'Shrike' rockets fuselage-mounted above the wheel wells to brake its descent, eight rearward-pointed

Making a slow descent

dorsal and two ventral fins on the rear fuselage, double-slotted flaps and extended ailerons, a new radome, a tail hook for landing aboard an aircraft carrier, and Combat Talon avionics, including a TF/TA radar, a defensive countermeasures suite, and a Doppler radar/GPS tie-in to the aircraft's inertial navigation system.

The test bed aircraft 74-2065 was ready for its first test flight on September 18, 1980, just three weeks after the project was initiated, and the first fully modified aircraft, 74-1683, was delivered on October 17 to TAB 1, a disused auxiliary airfield at Eglin Air Force Base, Florida. Between October 19 and October 28, numerous flights were made testing various aspects, including the double-slotted flaps system, which enabled the C-130 to fly at 85 knots on final approach at a very steep eight-degree glide slope. All aspects worked flawlessly, and a full profile test was scheduled for October 29. During the test, the Lockheed crew determined that the computer used to command the firing of the rockets during the landing sequence needed further calibration to perform the crucial firing sequence, and elected to manually input commands. The eight reverse-mounted (forward facing) ASROC rockets were situated in pairs on the upper curvature of the fuselage behind the cockpit, and at the mid-point of each side of the fuselage beneath the uppers. Testing had determined that the upper pairs, fired sequentially, could be ignited while still airborne (specifically, at 20 feet), whereas the lower pairs could only be fired after the aircraft was on the ground. The flight engineer, blinded by the firing of the upper deceleration rockets, thought the aircraft was on the runway and fired the lower set early, while the descent-braking rockets did not fire at all.

As a result, the aircraft's forward flight vector was reduced to zero, dropping it to the runway and tearing off the starboard wing between the third and fourth engines. During rollout the trailing wing ignited a fire, but crash response teams extinguished the fire within eight seconds of the aircraft stopping, enabling the crew to exit the aircraft without injury. 74-1683 was destroyed but most of its unique systems were salvaged. 74-1686 was nearly completed, but the defeat of Jimmy Carter by Ronald Reagan in the presidential election on November 4, 1980, and an Algerian-negotiated release plan, led to the cancellation of this rescue mission plan.

Forward-firing rockets ignite

A spectacular STOL take-off

Credible Sport II

The remaining airframes were stripped of their rocket modifications and 74-2065 returned to regular airlift duties. 74-1686, however, retained its other 'Credible Sport' STOL modifications and was sent to Robins Air Force Base, Georgia. There in July 1981 it was designated YMC-130H as the test bed for development of the MC-130 Combat Talon II, under the project name 'Credible Sport II'. Phase I was conducted between August 24 and November 11, 1981, to test minor modifications to improve aerodynamics, satisfy Combat Talon II prototype requirements on STOL performance, handling characteristics, and avionics, and to establish margins of safety. It also identified design deficiencies in the airframe and determined that the Credible Sport configuration was suitable only for its specific mission and did not have the safety margins necessary for peacetime operations. Phase II testing began June 15, 1982, continued through October 1982, which resulted in significant improvements in design, avionics, and equipment, and that the Combat Talon II design was ready for production. In 1988 74-1686 was placed on display at the Museum of Aviation at Robins Air Force Base in Warner Robins, Georgia.

74-1686 on display at the Museum of Aviation, Georgia

Aircraft Specifications

AC-130 GUNSHIP   PAGE 14

Close air support, air interdiction and force protection

Power Plant:	Four Allison T56-A-15 turboprop engines
Thrust:	4,910 shaft horsepower each engine
Wingspan:	132 feet, 7 inches (40.4 metres)
Length:	97 feet, 9 inches (29.8 metres)
Height:	38 feet, 6 inches (11.7 metres)
Speed:	300 mph
Range:	Approximately 1,300 nautical miles; unlimited with air refuelling
Ceiling:	25,000 feet (7,576 metres)
Max Take-off Weight:	155,000 pounds (69,750 kilograms)
Armament:	AC-130H: 40mm and 105mm cannons; AC-130U: 40mm and 105mm cannons and 25mm Gatling gun
Crew:	AC-130U - pilot, co-pilot, navigator, fire control officer, electronic warfare officer (officers) and flight engineer, TV operator, infrared detection set operator, loadmaster, four aerial gunners (enlisted)
Deployment Date:	AC-130H, 1972; AC-130U, 1995

MC-130E/H COMBAT TALON   PAGE 56

Infiltration, exfiltration and resupply of special operations forces

Power Plant:	Four Allison T56-A-15 turboprop engines
Thrust:	4,910 shaft horsepower each engine
Wingspan:	132 feet, 7 inches (40.4 metres)
Length MC-130E:	100 feet, 10 inches (30.7 metres)
Length MC-130H:	99 feet, 9 inches (30.4 metres)
Height:	38 feet, 6 inches (11.7 metres)
Speed:	300 mph
Load MC-130E:	53 troops, 26 paratroopers
Load MC-130H:	77 troops, 52 paratroopers or 57 litter patients
Ceiling:	33,000 feet (10,000 metres)
Max Take-off Weight:	155,000 pounds (69,750 kilograms)
Range:	2,700 nautical miles (4,344 kilometres); In-flight refuelling extends this to unlimited range
Crew MC-130E:	Two pilots, two navigators and an electronic warfare officer (officers); flight engineer, radio operator and two loadmasters (enlisted)
Crew MC-130H:	Two pilots, a navigator and electronic warfare officer (officers); flight engineer and two loadmasters (enlisted)

MC-130P COMBAT SHADOW   PAGE 90

Air refuelling for special operation forces helicopters

Power Plant:	Four Allison T56-A-15 turboprop engines
Thrust:	4,910 shaft horsepower each engine
Wingspan:	132 feet, 7 inches (40.4 metres)
Length:	98 feet, 9 inches (30.09 metres)
Height:	38 feet, 6 inches (11.7 metres)
Speed:	289 mph
Ceiling:	33,000 feet (10,000 metres)
Max Take-off Weight:	155,000 pounds (69,750 kilograms)
Range:	Beyond 4,000 miles
Crew:	Two pilots and two navigators (officers); flight engineer, communications systems operator and two loadmasters (enlisted)

MC-130W COMBAT SPEAR   PAGE 110

Infiltration, exfiltration and resupply of special operations forces; in-flight refuelling of special operations vertical lift assets

Power Plant:	Four Allison T56-A-15 turboprop engines
Thrust:	4,910 shaft horsepower each engine
Wingspan:	132 feet, 7 inches (40.4 metres)
Length:	98 feet, 9 inches (30.09 metres)
Height:	38 feet, 6 inches (11.7 metres)
Weight:	75,745 pounds (34,430 kilograms)
Max Take-off Weight:	155,000 pounds (69,750 kilograms)
Fuel Capacity:	44,240 pounds (20,108 kilograms)
Payload:	33,000 pounds (maximum) (14,969 kilograms)
Speed:	300 mph
Range:	1,208 miles (1,944 kilometres)
Ceiling:	33,000 feet (10,000 metres)
Crew:	Pilot, copilot, two navigators (officers), flight engineer and two loadmasters (enlisted)

MH/HH-60G PAVE HAWK   PAGE 112

Short-range combat rescue helicopter

Powerplant:	Two General Electric-GE-700/701C free-turbine turbo shaft engines
Thrust:	1,630 shaft horsepower per engine
Rotor Diameter:	53 ft 8 in (14.1 m)
Length:	64 ft 10 in (17.1 m)
Height:	16 ft 8 in (5.1 m)
Maximum Speed:	195 knots (224 mph, 360 km/h)
Ceiling:	14,000 ft (4,267 m)
Empty Weight:	16,000 lb (7,260 kg)
Range:	Internal tanks 373 miles (600.3 km), or with external tanks 508 miles (817.5 km)
Armament:	Two 7.62 mm mini-guns or Two 0.50 in machine guns
Crew:	4 (2 pilots, flight engineer, gunner)
Capacity:	6, 8-12 troops, plus litters and/or other cargo

MH-53 PAVE LOW   PAGE 38

Long-range infiltration, exfiltration and resupply of special operations forces in day, night or adverse weather conditions

Power Plant:	Two General Electric T64-GE-100 engines
Thrust:	4,330 shaft horsepower per engine
Rotary Diameter:	72 feet (21.9 metres)
Length:	88 feet (28 metres)
Height:	25 feet (7.6 metres)
Speed:	165 mph
Ceiling:	16,000 feet (4,876 metres)
Max Take-off Weight:	46,000 pounds (Emergency War Plan allows for 50,000 pounds)
Range:	600 nautical miles
Armament:	Combination of three 7.62 mini guns or three .50 caliber machine guns
Crew:	Two pilots (officers); Two flight engineers and two aerial gunners (enlisted)

EC-130 COMMANDO SOLO   PAGE 102

Psychological operations and information operations

Power Plant:	AE2100D3 six-blade turboprops
Thrust:	6,000 shaft horsepower each engine
Wingspan:	132.6 feet (40.3 metres)
Length:	97.75 feet (29.7 metres)
Height:	38.8 feet (11.8 metres)
Cruise speed:	335 mph
Ceiling:	28,000 feet (8,534 metres)
Max Take-off Weight:	164,000 pounds (74,390 kilograms)
Range:	2,300 nautical miles unrefuelled
Crew:	Pilot, copilot, flight systems officer, mission systems officer; loadmaster, five electronic communications systems operators

(© Rick Llinares)

CV-22 OSPREY   PAGE 76

Special operations forces long-range infiltration, exfiltration, and resupply

Power Plant:	Two Rolls Royce-Allison AE1107C turbo shaft engines
Thrust:	More than 6,200 shaft horsepower per engine
Wingspan:	84 feet, 7 inches (25.8 metres)
Length:	57 feet, 4 inches (17.4 metres)
Height:	22 feet, 1 inch (6.73 metres)
Rotary Diameter:	38 feet (11.6 metres)
Speed:	277 miles per hour
Ceiling:	25,000 feet (7,620 metres)
Max Take-off Weight:	Vertical 52,870 pounds (23,982 kilograms)
Max Take-off Weight:	Rolling 60,500 pounds (27,443 kilograms)
Range:	2,100 nautical miles with internal auxiliary fuel tanks
Payload:	24 troops (seated), 32 troops (floor loaded) or 10,000 pounds of cargo
Crew:	Four (pilot, copilot and two enlisted flight engineers)

Firing off a volley of flares – a colourful sight!